PARACHUTE PLAY

By
Liz and Dick Wilmes

Art
Janet McDonnell

A  Publication
38W567 Brindlewood Ln
Elgin, IL 60123

ISBN 0-943452-30-9

ART

Text Illustrations	Cover Graphics	Text and Graphics Layout
Janet McDonnell	David Van Delinder	Greg Wilmes
Arlington Heights, Illinois	Studio IVV	Noblesville, Indiana
	Elgin, Illinois	

SPECIAL THANKS

to Jane Flynn who has contributed several of her favorite parachute play activities and songs. Enjoy them with your children

PUBLISHED BY

Building Blocks

38W567 Brindlewood
Elgin, Illinois 60123

DISTRIBUTED BY

Gryphon House	Consortium Book Sales	Monarch Books
P.O. Box 207	1045 Westgate Drive	5000 Dufferin St., Unit K
Beltsville, MD 20704	St. Paul, MN 5514	Downsview, Ontario
		Canada M3H 5T5
(Educational Stores and Catalog)	(U.S. Book Trade)	(All Canadian Orders)

Dedicated To:

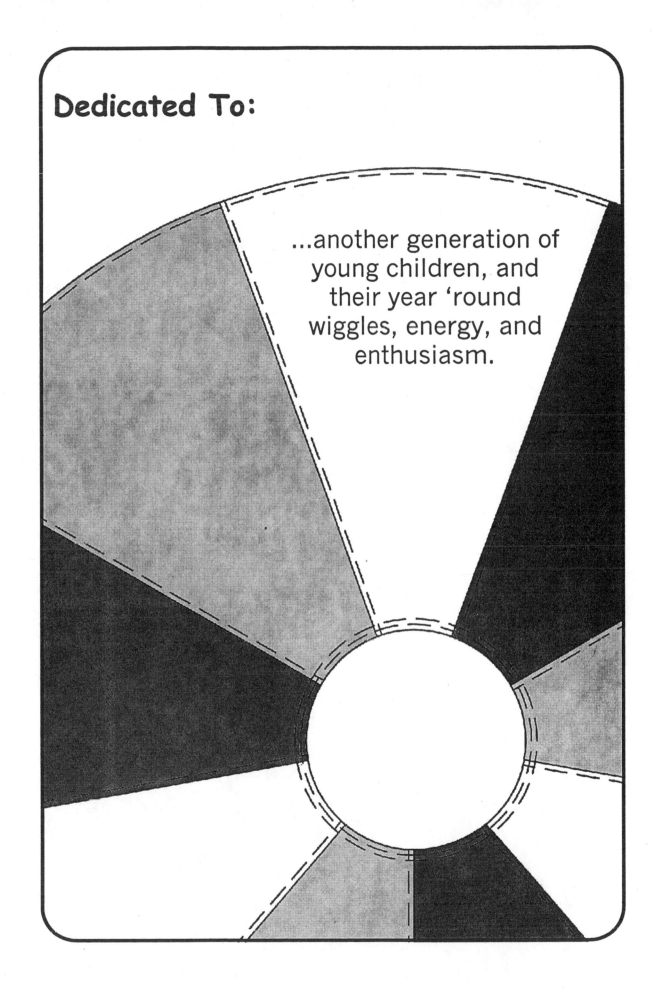

...another generation of young children, and their year 'round wiggles, energy, and enthusiasm.

CONTENTS

Holiday And Seasonal Games

Cool-Down Activities

Building Blocks Resources

INTRODUCTION

Why Play With Parachutes

Parachutes are one of the most versatile pieces of equipment that you can use with young children. Through the wide variety of activities, you can help children increase their ability to:

* Follow Directions.
* Use Language.
* Join Group Activities.
* Socialize.
* Develop Small Muscle Control.
* Strengthen Large Muscles.
* Remain in Control During Very Active Play.

Keeping Things Under Control

People often think that parachute play is a 'wild' and 'uncontrolled' activity. Parachute play can be and should be a controlled, very active, and a really fun type of activity.

When doing parachute play, keep several things in mind. They will help you and the children enjoy your parachute play even more.

* Begin and end your parachute playtime with the parachute in a bunched-up position.

* Use the *"STOP"* direction to control the flow of every activity.

* Always take time to rest during and between activities as children tire. Use these rest periods to talk about how the parachute looks and feels. *Is it making noise? What body parts are the children using in a particular activity?*

* Vary the games and activities by changing body positions, handgrips, parachute positions, and parachute motions.

* Use slow, quiet activities to conclude every session.

How To Use <u>PARACHUTE PLAY</u>

<u>PARACHUTE PLAY</u> is divided into 6 sections:

- ✳ At a Glance
- ✳ 8 Basic Sessions
- ✳ Warm-Up Exercises
- ✳ Year 'Round Games
- ✳ Holiday and Seasonal Games
- ✳ Cool-Down Activities.

AT A GLANCE

A brief summary of parachute grips, positions, and movements to quickly get the children involved in <u>PARACHUTE PLAY</u>.

8 BASIC SESSIONS

It is very important that you do the BASIC SESSIONS with the children before you enjoy any of the other exercises, games and/or activities in PARACHUTE PLAY. Each of the 8 SESSIONS is designed for 10-15 minutes of parachute fun. This is enough time to learn new skills, have fun, and not get too tired.

After a wide variety of simple activities in these SESSIONS, the children will have:

- ✳ Learned different ways to hold and move the chute.
- ✳ Developed more strength.
- ✳ Learned how to control balls on the parachute.
- ✳ Experienced going under the chute.
- ✳ Developed an understanding of group games.

WARM-UP EXERCISES

Warm-Up Exercises provide a good beginning to parachute play. They help children remember:

* Different parachute holds and movements.
* How to work together.
* How to move their bodies to coordinate with the chute.
* How to control balls, ropes, beanbags, and other props on the chute.
* What it feels like to go under the chute.

YEAR 'ROUND, SEASONAL and HOLIDAY GAMES

Have fun playing a wide variety of PARACHUTE GAMES. Children will play on the edge, under, and around the chute. They will use all types of balls, short and long ropes, beanbags, balloons, bells, streamers, and other props.

Each game has a chart of beginning information so you know how to hold and move the chute, what extra equipment you may need, and different themes that are natural to each game.

Each game also tells you which WARM-UP EXERCISE and COOL-DOWN ACTIVITY is most appropriate. Start and end with these.

COOL-DOWN ACTIVITIES

Children have been enjoying lots of active play on the parachute. Before you fold up the parachute, do a quiet activity. Let the children calm down, relax, and take a breath. All these activities should be done slowly, with very quiet voices.

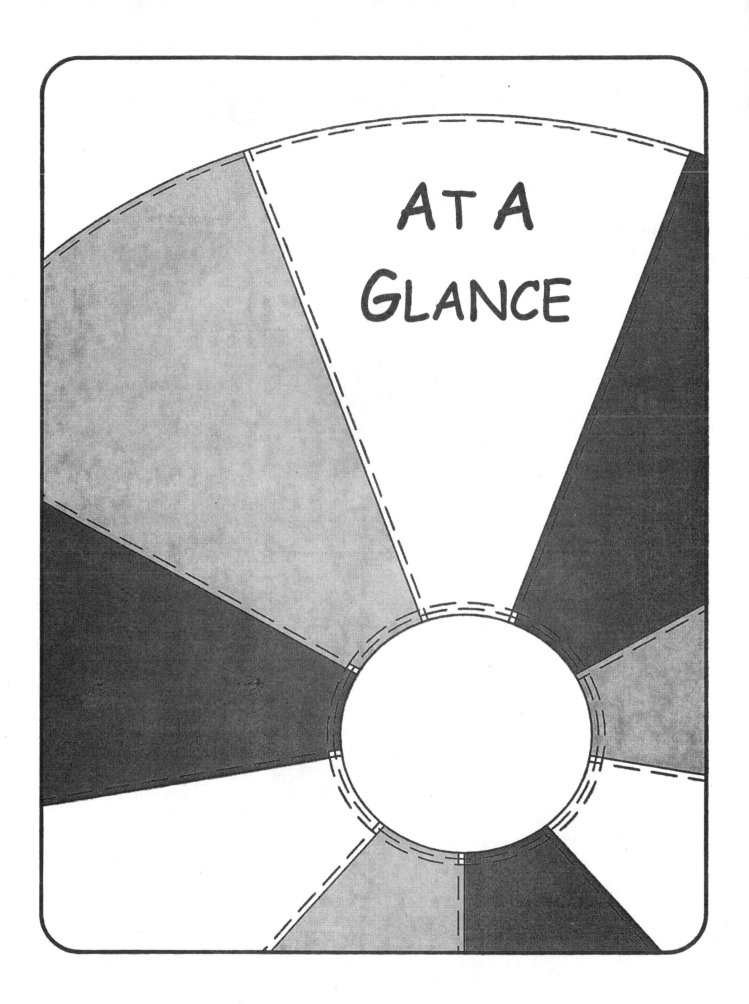

PARACHUTE GRIPS

INTRODUCTION

There are four basic ways to grip a parachute. Children should learn to use the first two grips before they are introduced to the last two.

THUMBS-UP

In the Thumbs-Up grip the fingers are under the parachute and the thumbs are visible over the chute. In other words, the fists are holding onto the parachute underneath it and the thumbs are up, holding onto the parachute from above.

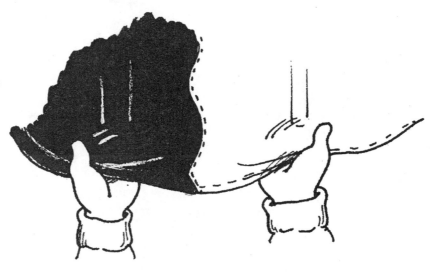

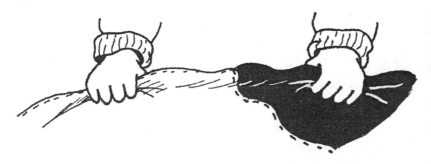

THUMBS-DOWN

The Thumbs-Down grip is the opposite of Thumbs-Up. The thumbs are holding the parachute underneath and the four fingers are visible over the parachute. Thus, in this grip, the fingers are up and the thumbs are down.

THUMBS-UP — THUMBS-DOWN

As was stated above, this grip is more difficult and should be used for variety after the children are comfortable with the first two.

To do this grip, have the children grab the parachute using the Thumbs-Up grip with one hand and the Thumbs-Down grip with the other one.

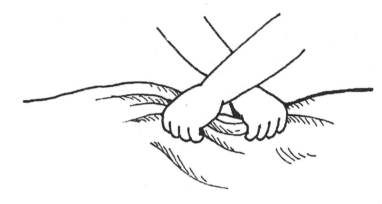

ARMS CROSSED

This grip is another variation of the first two grips and can be used for diversity in many of the activities. The children should cross their arms over each other and grab the parachute with either the Thumbs-Up or Thumbs-Down grip.

FIRMLY HOLD THE PARACHUTE

In addition to using one of the four grips, the children must learn to firmly hold the parachute.

To Do This:

1. They first need to grab a handful of the parachute fabric.

   This is difficult in the beginning because their hands are small, their muscles are not very strong, and the parachute fabric is slippery.

2. Secondly they need to remember to keep their fists closed.

   Again, this is hard in the beginning, because children's hands easily get tired and because they get so involved with the activity they forget to hold on.

   Consequently the parachute can get jerked out of their hands.

15

BODY POSITIONS

INTRODUCTION

Many parachute games can be done from all three body positions. Depending on the activity, there is usually a best or most comfortable position from which to enjoy each game. Start with that position and then do the activity again from one of the other two positions. After you have tried it from at least two different body positions, talk about the two approaches. See if the children felt any differences.

1. SITTING
AROUND THE PARACHUTE

Though there are many ways to sit on the floor, cross-legged is the most appropriate for the majority of parachute activities. For some games, the children will, however, sit with their legs straight out.

The sitting position is the least active of all the positions, because the children are most limited in their movements and a minimal amount of air is trapped under the parachute. As you will soon discover, sitting is usually the least fun and not used as often as kneeling and standing.

It is, however, a great position from which to teach most activities. The children are more able to concentrate on the directions from a sitting position than they are from a kneeling or standing one.

2. KNEELING
AROUND THE PARACHUTE

As with the sitting position, the kneeling position is a great one from which to teach a new activity or vary an old one. Because the parachute is higher off the ground than in the sitting position, more air is trapped under the chute to get a fuller, higher effect from the parachute movements. Because the children are on their knees, they can move more freely.

When kneeling, children can either kneel up straight or rest back on their heels. The type of activity will determine the position.

3. STANDING
AROUND THE PARACHUTE

As you and your group of children feel more and more comfortable with parachute play, you will discover that you do many of the activities from a standing position and use the sitting and kneeling positions for the variations.

To fully enjoy any activity from this position, be sure that the children understand the directions. If you find that they do not, switch to one of the other positions and do the activity from there.

In the standing position, the greatest amount of air is under the parachute and the children are able to move freely in many ways.

PARACHUTE POSITIONS

INTRODUCTION

Though the parachute can be held in any position in relationship to the body, there are generally three places from which most parachute activities originate.

For each game, there is usually a most appropriate position and the other two are used for variation and added excitement or challenge when you repeat the games. Other times, more than one position is used during a game. The activity may begin in a certain place and switch to another position depending on the flow of the activity.

Because of the constant movement of the parachute, the children must be very familiar with how to hold the parachute in the three main positions.

1. WAY UP HIGH

When holding the parachute in this position, children extend their arms over their heads so the parachute is floating above the group. Though this is really fun and an exciting way to hold the parachute, it is also the most tiring. During activities, which use this position, you must have many opportunities to rest throughout the flow of the game.

18

2. WAY DOWN LOW

When the children hold the parachute low, it usually floats around their knees. If it floats much lower than that, you will not get enough air under the parachute to get the effects you want.

Doing activities with the parachute in this position is usually very quieting for the children. It is great to use this position while doing the last activity or a variation in the sequence. By using it, the children will most often finish the parachute play in a calm manner and be able to transition to the next activity of the day with no excess energy.

3. IN THE MIDDLE

Of the three parachute positions, this one is used the most and is the most comfortable to maintain. The parachute is held right around the waist. From there children can enjoy many of the activities as well as easily move the parachute to higher lower positions.

RESTING

Other than the three basic parachute positions, there is also the resting position. Parachute play can be very active. As you enjoy the different games, you will need to periodically take a break. During rest times, continue to hold onto the parachute (unless otherwise instructed) whether you are sitting, kneeling, or standing. Usually it is most relaxing if the children simply let their arms hang loosely in front of them.

The more the children use the parachute, the stronger they will become and their need for rest breaks diminishes. Use the rest periods to talk about what is happening to the parachute and how the children feel.

PARACHUTE MOVEMENTS

INTRODUCTION

By moving their arms, hands, and wrists in different combinations, a group of people can make a parachute wiggle in a variety of ways. The different effects, which are created, are used in various parachute activities. There are five basic movements. Enjoy these first and then create your own variations and new movements.

1. WAVE

There are two types of WAVE movements.

Rippling Wave

1. The first one is a simple both arms up-both arms down motion. Each person does this up and down motion as an individual. He does not do it in unison with the group. This type of movement causes a RIPPLING WAVE in the chute. It is a very basic motion and used often.

Giant Wave

2. The second type of waving movement is once again a both arms up-both arms down movement, but this time the group must do it in unison; that is, everyone up-everyone-down. Instead of the rippling effect caused by the first type of waving movement, the parachute billows high in the air and creates a GIANT WAVE. This type of waving movement is more spectacular than the first and requires more control of the parachute.

2. JERK

The JERK is a side-to-side movement of the parachute. Hold the parachute with two hands. There are two ways to do the JERK. The type of parachute game you play will dictate which type of JERK you'll use.

Together

1. You can do this movement in rhythm with everyone jerking right and left, continuing right-left, right-left, right-left.

Individually

2. You can also do this movement more randomly with each person individually jerking right and left.

3. FLIP-FLOP

In the FLIP-FLOP each person alternates his arms, so that when the right arm is up, the left one is down. When doing the FLIP-FLOP, the parachute wiggles and jiggles randomly. It is one the children's favorites, especially when doing it very quickly.

21

4. TAUT

When holding the parachute TAUT, everyone pulls back on the chute until it is completely spread out and has no slack in it. The type of exercise or activity you are going to play, will dictate how hard you will pull on the parachute.

In the beginning, young children will only be able to pull slightly. As they learn how to tightly hold onto the chute and have more strength, they will be able to pull the chute more taut.

5. SNAP

The SNAP is probably the most difficult movement. To do it effectively, the children should be strong enough to hold tightly onto the parachute and be able to carefully listen to directions.

The SNAP is mainly a wrist action. Hanging on firmly, flick both wrists in unison with a quick up-down motion; then stop. As the children flick their wrists, they should also pull slightly back on the chute. This snapping motion takes practice. When it is done effectively the chute jumps and makes a cracking sound.

PARACHUTE PLAY
At A Glance

START WITH A "BUNCHED –UP" CHUTE

PARACHUTE GRIPS
1. Thumbs-Up
2. Thumbs-Down
3. Thumb-Up – Thumb-Down
4. Arms Crossed

BODY POSITIONS
1. Sitting
2. Kneeling
3. Standing

PARACHUTE POSITIONS
1. Way Up High
2. Way Down Low
3. In the Middle

PARACHUTE MOVEMENTS
1. Wave
2. Jerk
3. Flip-Flop
4. Taut
5. Snap

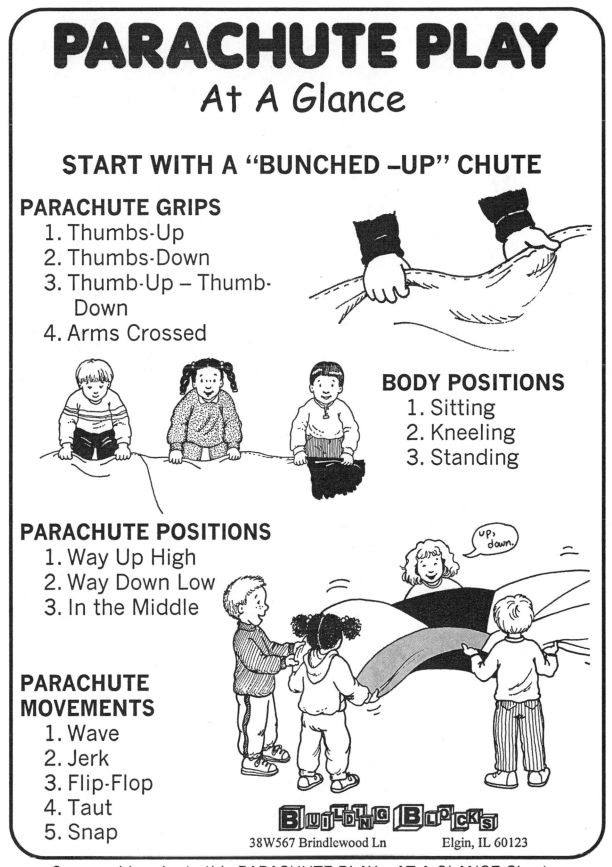

BUILDING BLOCKS

38W567 Brindlewood Ln   Elgin, IL 60123

Copy and Laminate this PARACHUTE PLAY – AT A GLANCE Chart.
Post It In Your Large Motor Area

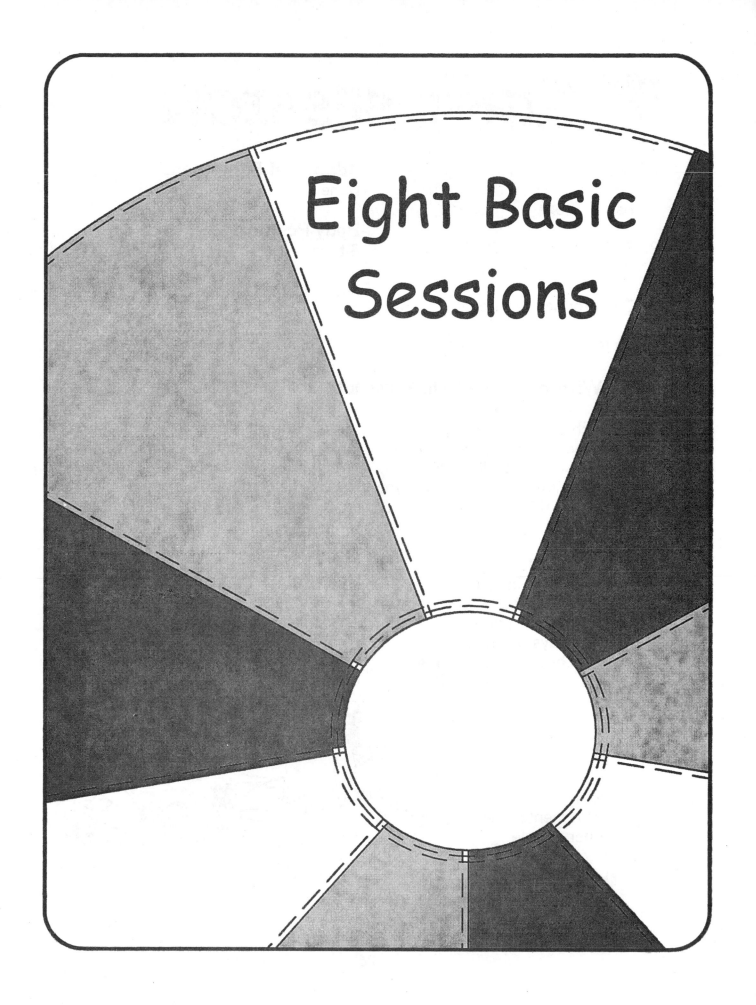

Eight Basic Sessions

FIRST SESSION

Objectives:

1. To introduce children to the parachute.

2. To introduce the Thumbs-Up grip.

3. To introduce the Wave.

4. To learn the *"STOP"* direction.

Additional Equipment:
None

Body Position:
Sitting

Hand Grips:
Thumbs-Up (two hands)

Begin With a Bunched-Up Parachute

Each time you enjoy parachute play with the children, begin with the parachute in a bunched-up position. Before the children come to the area where you'll be doing your parachute activities, bunch-up the parachute, being sure that the edges of the chute are clearly visible, so that the children can easily grip the edge of the chute when it's time to begin.

As the children arrive in the area have them sit around the bunched-up parachute. By always beginning parachute play in this manner, the children are ready to talk about the activities they will be doing, demonstrate holds, movements, and other simple directions. When the parachute is bunched-up, there is less opportunity to move the chute before you've given them directions.

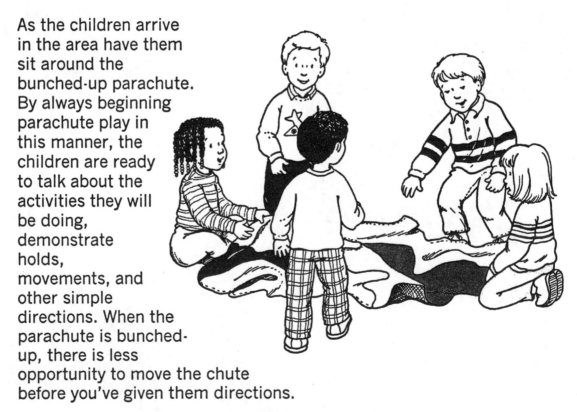

26

Introduce the THUMBS-UP GRIP

While the children are sitting around the bunched-up chute, have them hold up their hands. Do several fingerplays to loosen up their hands and fingers.

10 LITTLE FINGERS

I have 10 little fingers
They all belong to me.
I can make them do things
Do you want to see?

I can close them up tight.
I can open them up wide.
I can hold them up high.
I can hold them down low.
I can wave them to and fro,
And I can hold them just so.

FINGERS
by Dick Wilmes

These are my 10 fingers.
They do whatever I say.
They help me when I'm eating.
They help me when I play.

Sometimes they work together.
Sometimes they work apart.
You can do so many things with them,
Can you think of one to start?

(Let the children name what they do with their fingers.)

After you've enjoyed several fingerplays have the children once again hold up both of their hands. While their hands are in the air (not holding the chute) have the children make fists with their fingers and palms and turn them so they face the ceiling. At the same time, have them point their thumbs to the ceiling. This is the THUMBS-UP grip.

While still sitting around the bunched-up chute have the children hold the parachute with the Thumbs-Up grip. Tell them to grab a handful of the parachute fabric so that their fingers will be hiding under the chute and their thumbs will be peeking over the chute. When they are all holding the chute, have them look at another child and wiggle their thumbs at the person. Pick another child and wiggle at him.

Put the chute down and have the children shake their hands and wiggle their fingers. After the short rest, grab the chute again with the Thumbs-Up grip. Sing the first verse of WHERE IS THUMBKIN. In the last two lines, instead of singing *"Run away — Run away,"* sing *"Hold on tight — Hold on tight."* As you sing those lines, have the children lay their thumbs on top of the parachute and hold it. This song is a great way to begin parachute play. It helps the children all grab the chute together, is upbeat, and sets a good mood for parachute play. Use it often!

WHERE IS THUMBKIN?

Where is thumbkin?
Where is thumbkin?
Here I am. *(Wiggle thumbs above chute.)*
Here I am.

How are you today, sir? *(Wiggle one thumb at the other thumb.)*
Very well I thank you. *(Wiggle other thumb at first one.)*
Hold on tight. *(Grab chute with one thumb.)*
Hold on tight. *(Grab chute with other thumb.)*

Introduce the WAVE

Now that the children are familiar with one type of grip, have them quietly stand and hold the chute Thumbs-Up. While holding the chute, walk backwards until it is fully open. Sit down and lay the chute on the ground. Explain the WAVE as a motion in which each person moves both arms up and then both arms down. The group does not have to move together. Each person moves his arms as an individual. Do it first without the chute. Have the children say, *"Up - down"* to themselves as they move their arms. This up and down rhythm will cause the parachute to form shallow wave-like motions — ripples.

Now grab the chute Thumbs-Up. Enjoy doing the WAVE slowly. If you feel the children understand the movement, do it a little faster and then very fast. Return to calm by waving the parachute slower. Rest.

"STOP"

Several times while the children are enjoying the wave, firmly say, *"Stop!"* When you do, the children should immediately quit. To enjoy parachute activities, they need to follow this direction.

Have the children repeat the wave from a standing position. Remember to use the Thumbs-Up grip and give the *"STOP"* direction often. Begin and end the movement slowly as you did from a sitting position.

Play FREEZE

Using the Thumbs-Up grip and the wave motion, enjoy playing FREEZE. Put a musical record on the record player. As the music plays, the child dance and wave the chute. When you stop the music, say *"STOP"* in a firm voice. When the children hear you, they should stop dancing and waving the parachute. Begin the record again and continue playing FREEZE. When the record is over, change to a song with a different tempo and play again. This activity is an excellent way to reinforce the *"STOP"* direction.

END

After you have played FREEZE several times, the children will probably be tired. At this point, have them hold the parachute using the Thumbs-Up grip. Enjoy several slow waves to quiet down. Say, *"STOP."* Then have the children slowly walk the chute back to its bunched-up shape and sit down around it. Talk a little about this first parachute play experience.

29

SECOND SESSION

Objectives:

1. To review the Thumbs-Up grip.

2. To review the Wave.

3. To introduce the Thumbs-Down grip.

4. To begin Movements with the parachute

Additional Equipment:
None

Body Positions:
Sitting and Standing

Hand Grips:
Thumbs-Up and Thumbs-Down (two hands)

Begin

Start your activities by bunching-up the parachute in the middle of your empty area. The children should sit around it in the beginning. At first have them grab the parachute with both hands using the Thumbs-Up grip as they have previously done. Look at each child's grip. Remind all the children that their thumbs should be peeking over the parachute and their fingers hiding under it. While they are holding the chute with this grip, have them say good morning or good afternoon to their friends by wiggling their thumbs at each other and saying *"Hi."*

Introduce the THUMBS-DOWN GRIP

Now introduce the second grip. The THUMBS-DOWN grip is the opposite of Thumbs-Up. In this position the children put their four fingers over the chute and their thumbs under the chute. Do it in the air first and then grab the parachute. While gripping the parachute in this manner, have them wiggle their fingers at a friend across the parachute. Then sing the

last four verses of WHERE IS THUMBKIN. Remember to change the last 2 lines to *"Hold on tight — Hold on tight."* Each time have the children grip the chute with the finger they are singing about. At the end, they will be using the Thumbs-Down grip.

MOVING and CHANTING

Walk. Walk. Walk

Until now the children have done activities from a fairly stationary position. Now you're going to introduce movement while gripping the parachute.

Begin with walking. Have the children grab the chute with the Thumbs-Down grip and begin walking clockwise in a circle. As you walk, everyone chant, *"Walk, Walk, Walk..."* to the rhythm of your stride. When you decide you want to change the speed, say *"STOP."* Walk at a different pace, maybe a little faster. As you walk to this quicker rhythm, remember to chant *"Walk, Walk, Walk..."* as you go.

Not only can you vary the speeds with which you move, you can also change the movements. Once the children have learned to easily walk at different speeds, try sliding, galloping, or running. Use the *"STOP"* command between movements. Remember you can do any of these movements at different speeds. You can also use a Thumbs-Up or Thumbs-Down grip. No matter what movement, grip, or speed you use, always chant. This chant:

- ❋ Helps keep everyone moving at the same pace
- ❋ Assists with control, and
- ❋ Definitely makes the activity more fun because the children's whole bodies are involved.

The last movement should be tiptoeing. By ending with a slow movement, the activity itself will quiet the children. Chant *"Tiptoe, Tiptoe, Tiptoe..."* in a quiet, almost whisper voice. You will feel the children relaxing as you move.

END: Have them tiptoe the parachute slowly to the middle.

THIRD SESSION

Objectives:

1. To review the two Basic Grips.

2. To review the Wave at different speeds.

3. To introduce Kneeling with the parachute.

4. To introduce 3 Parachute Positions.

5. To use a Ball with the parachute.

Additional Equipment:
Beach ball (Small size is best.)

Body Position:
Kneeling and Standing

Hand Grips:
Thumbs-Up and Thumbs-Down (two hands)

Begin

The children will begin by sitting around the bunched-up chute. Have them pretend that they are holding a parachute with the Thumbs-Up grip. (Quickly scan the group to be sure everyone's thumbs are Up and their fists are closed and facing the ceiling.) With this grip have them pretend to wave the parachute slowly, a little faster, and now very fast. Switch to a Thumbs-Down grip and pretend to wave the chute again.

Introduce the KNEELING POSITION

The children have enjoyed parachute activities from both a sitting and standing position. KNEELING is a third body position. In this position, the children will have more fun with the parachute movements than from the sitting position.

Have the children Kneel around the bunched-up chute. Have them grab the parachute with the Thumbs-Up grip. Now switch to Thumbs-Down. It takes time to make the switch, so be sure to give the children a sufficient pause to reverse their hands. Switch several times.

32

Introduce the 3 PARACHUTE POSITIONS

While standing around the bunched-up chute, introduce the 3 basic parachute positions:

- ❋ Down low by their knees.
- ❋ In the middle by their waists.
- ❋ Way up high above their heads.

Have them pretend to grab the parachute with the Thumbs-Up grip. Now have them pretend to move it one time into each of the 3 positions. After this, play SIMON SAYS (no tricking), again pretending to hold the parachute.

SIMON SAYS, *"Thumbs-Up, kneel down and hold the parachute above your head. STOP."*

SIMON SAYS, *"Thumbs-Up, sit down, hold the parachute at your waist. STOP.*

SIMON SAYS, *"Thumbs-Down, stand up, hold the parachute at your knees. STOP."*

SIMON SAYS, *"Listen carefully. This time grab the chute Thumbs-Up. Stand and move the parachute to your waist. Walk backwards to spread the parachute all the way out."*

Play SIMON SAYS

While standing with the chute fully spread, continue playing SIMON SAYS, only this time with the parachute in your hands. (Give commands at an appropriate pace for your group. As you do, walk around the chute helping any child who needs assistance.) After you've given 6-7 commands, transition to the next activity by commanding,

SIMON SAYS, *"Thumbs-Up, kneel down, and put the parachute at your waist."*

33

Introduce the BEACH BALL

While you're introducing the BEACH BALL, have the children sit back on their legs and relax their arms, but continue to hold the parachute with the Thumbs-Up grip. This is a fairly relaxing position and will give the children an opportunity to rest their arms.

Hold up the beach ball. Tell the children that you are going to toss the ball onto the parachute. When you do they are going to use the slow wave motion and gently roll the ball around the parachute trying to keep it on the chute. If the ball rolls off, and it probably will, a child should retrieve it and toss it back onto the chute. (Name the "Ball Chaser" ahead of time.)

Play AROUND AND AROUND — BACK AND FORTH

To begin playing, say *"Let's hold the parachute Thumbs-Up, kneel straight, and hold the chute at our waists."* When everyone is ready, place the ball on the parachute and let the children begin to slowly roll it around. Periodically say, *"STOP"* and then let the children continue to roll the ball. After rolling it around, roll it back and forth across the chute.

Play SIMON SAYS

After they have become comfortable with having an object on the parachute, say *"STOP"* and take the ball off. Vary the game in this manner. Use a Thumbs-Down grip, continue to kneel, but now give specific directions to each child to roll the beach ball to. Do this by again playing SIMON SAYS. Get ready. Put the ball in front of a child.

SIMON SAYS, *"Anglea, roll the ball to Paul."*

SIMON SAYS, *"Paul, roll the ball to Riley."*

Continue.

When rolling the ball from one person to another, the children around the person with the ball will all gently lift the chute up in the direction of the other child. As the ball rolls across the chute towards the designated child, others will need to cooperate, directing the ball toward the right child by using the slow waving motion.

END

Conclude your parachute play by using 3 more commands:

SIMON SAYS, *"Eric, roll the ball to me"* (teacher).

SIMON SAYS, *"Stand up, slowly walk the parachute to the middle, and bunch it up on the floor."*

When the children are in the middle,

SIMON SAYS, *"Tiptoe to lunch"* (or whatever the next activity will be.)

FOURTH SESSION

Objectives:
1. To use the Wave in the 3 different Parachute Positions.

2. To introduce the Jerk.

3. To introduce holding the parachute with One Hand.

Additional Equipment:
Washable Marker, Beach Ball

Body Position:
Standing

Hand Grips:
Thumbs-Up and Thumbs-Down (two hands and one hand)

Begin

While the children are sitting around the bunched-up chute, enjoy several fingerplays to loosen up their fingers and hands.

BUSY FINGERS
(tune: Mulberry Bush)
     by Liz Wilmes

This the way my fingers stand,
Fingers stand, fingers stand,
This is the way my fingers stand,
So early in the morning.

This is the way my fingers dance,
Fingers dance, fingers dance,
This is the way they dance about,
So early in the morning.

This is the way my fingers bend,
Fingers bend, fingers bend,
This is the way my fingers bend,
So early in the morning.

This is the way my fingers rest,
Fingers rest, fingers rest,
This is the way my fingers rest,
So early in the morning.

COUNTING

One, two, three, four
I can even count some more.
Five, six, seven, eight
All my fingers stand up
     straight.
Nine, ten are my thumb men.

36

After the fingerplays, have the children stand, turn their backs to the parachute and grab the parachute with a Thumbs-Up grip. Walk forward with the parachute until it is fully spread out. Then turn around, use a Thumbs-Up grip and hold the parachute at their knees. To check everyone's grip have them wiggle their thumbs at each other.

WAVING

While in this position, have the children begin waving the chute slowly. As they wave it, sing ROW, ROW, ROW YOUR BOAT to the rhythm of their wave.

Have them move the parachute to their waists. Toss a beach ball onto the parachute. Pretend that the ball is a boat and that a storm is coming up. The boat is being tossed around the water. (Wave the chute a little faster.) The storm continues to build up and the boat is really being rocked around. (Wave very fast.)

All storms eventually subside and so does this one. Soon the boat is gently rocking once again. (Wave the parachute slowly.) Sing ROW, ROW, ROW YOUR BOAT slowly and quietly.

Rest. While doing so, talk about waving the parachute at different speeds. *"How do their arms feel? What speed was the most fun? Why?"*

After your discussion, have the children grab the parachute Thumbs-Up, hold it above their heads, and wave it slowly for a short time. While they are waving the chute, have them look at their friends under the chute. Lower the chute and rest. Remember that holding the chute above their heads is very tiring, so only do it for a short time.

Introduce the JERK

As opposed to the wave, which is an up and down motion of the parachute, the JERK is a side-to-side motion. Have the children grab the parachute Thumbs-Down. Quickly go around the group and mark an "X" on everyone's right hand and an "O" on their left hand. (If all the children can differentiate their left and right hands, this step is unnecessary.)

Holding tightly to the chute, have everyone JERK the chute in the direction of this "X" hand (right), now to their "O" hand (left), back to the right and then to the left. *"STOP."* When the group understands the motion, jerk the chute at different speeds. The children should chant the word *"jerk"* as they do it. Range from a very slow movement to a rapid one.

Toss a beach ball onto the chute. Wave the chute and then discuss what happened to the ball. Keeping the ball on the chute, do the jerk movement at various speeds. *"What happened to the beach ball when the parachute moved side-to-side? Did the ball move the same when the parachute was waved and jerked?"*

38

Introduce HOLDING THE PARACHUTE WITH ONE HAND

During a previous parachute session, the children held the parachute with two hands and did simple movements as they rotated in the same direction in a circle. From the standing position and Thumbs-Down have them hold the parachute waist high and enjoy several of the movements again — walk, gallop, run, and then a slow tiptoe. They should remember to chant as they move. Say *"STOP"* between movements.

Now that their minds and bodies have been refreshed, have the children stop. Tell them that they are going to continue doing movements, but now they are going to grip the parachute with only one hand. Have them all face the same direction and grab the chute with either their *"X"* or *"O"* hand using a Thumbs-Down grip.

Begin walking at an average pace holding the parachute waist high. (Remember to chant, *"Walk, Walk, Walk..."*) After a little while say, *"STOP."* Switch hands, use the Thumbs-Up grip and begin walking again. They should remember to hold on tightly.

Continue enjoying different simple movements along with the appropriate chant. Remember to switch directions for variety. Give the children enough time to make all the adjustments before they begin each new movement.

END

After the last movement, have them once again grab the parachute with both hands. Lift the parachute above your heads and begin to slowly walk to the middle. About halfway there, have the children lower the parachute to their waists and walk the rest of the way.

Lay the parachute down and sit around it. Call out each child's name. Have him tell the rest of the children where he's going next and then he may leave the area and continue with the next activity.

FIFTH SESSION

Objectives:
1. To review all of the parachute Grips, Speeds, Positions, and Movements
2. To introduce the Giant Wave In Unison.

Additional Equipment:
None

Body Positions:
Standing and Sitting

Hand Grips:
Thumbs-Up and Thumbs-Down (One Hand — Two Hands)

Begin

Sit around the parachute. When everyone is ready, simply have the children shake their hands and wiggle their fingers. Say *"STOP."* Then give them specific directions, such as:

* *"Wiggle your fingers way up high."*
* *"Shake your hands near your knees."*
* *"Make the Thumbs-Up grip and wiggle your thumbs."*

* Last Direction – *"Grab the parachute with the Thumbs-Up grip, stand, hold it above your head, and walk backwards until it is fully spread out."*

When it is completely out, have them lower the chute to their waists.

40

Play FOLLOW THE LEADER

The children have learned many ways to manipulate the parachute in a short period of time.

- ❀ Two ways to Grip it,
- ❀ How to Wave it.
- ❀ How to Jerk it.
- ❀ How to Wave and Jerk at Different Speeds.
- ❀ How to move with it using either a One Hand or a Two Hand Grip.
- ❀ How to enjoy activities from a Sitting, Standing, and Kneeling Position.
- ❀ How to hold the parachute in Three Basic Places — at their Knees, Waists, and Over Their Heads.

Using different combinations of skills the children know, play FOLLOW THE LEADER. The teacher should be the Leader. The children should watch what grip is used, where the parachute is being held, what body position the teacher chooses, and then the specific movement. Do the movement for a while, say "STOP" and then create a new combination. Enjoy seven or eight combinations with the children. Remember to go at a pace that is comfortable for the children.

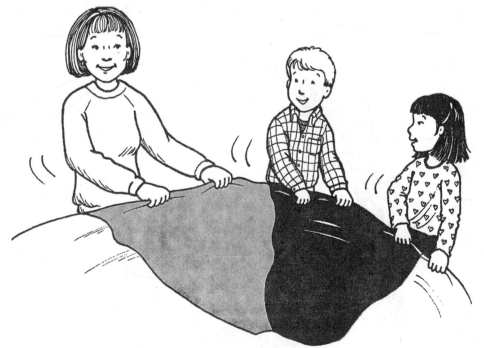

Introduce the WAVE IN UNISON

Until now the children have been using a both arms up and both arms down waving motion, as individuals, to create RIPPLE WAVES. When they rolled the beach ball around and back and forth, they were aware of working together with several other children. Now, however, the group will take a big step in parachute play. They will all move their arms together. All of the children will go up together and then down together — thus creating a GIANT WAVE.

While in the sitting position have the children grab the parachute using the Thumbs-Up grip. Tell them they are going to move the parachute together. When you say, *"Up"* they should lift the parachute about chest high. When you say, *"Down"* they should lower it. Do this *"Up together — Down together"* motion several times. Talk about what happens to the parachute when they all move in unison.

To create an even more dramatic effect of this movement, have the children WAVE IN UNISON from a standing position. First have them take several steps to the middle, creating a little slack in the parachute. Then begin to wave it. In the beginning, be careful not to let the parachute get too high, for the children may not be strong enough to control it. After awhile they'll all feel comfortable as the parachute forms giant waves over their heads. To get the chute even higher, create slack by having the children take several more steps towards the middle.

END

Before you WAVE for the last time, tell the children that the next time they wave the parachute over their heads, you will give the verbal signal, *"Let go."* They should watch it float to the ground. When it is on the ground, have them grab it, walk it to the middle and sit down.

This has been an exciting and strenuous day with the parachute. Before they leave, play a quiet record. As it is playing, have the children slowly wave the bunched-up chute. Then whisper, *"John, go to art. Shannon, your turn to play with the blocks"* and so on until all the children have left the parachute and are involved in other activities.

SIXTH SESSION

Objectives:
1. To review the Wave.

2. To review the Jerk.

3. To introduce the Flip-Flop.

Additional Equipment:
Beach Ball, Washable Marker

Body Position:
Standing

Hand Grips:
Thumbs-Up and Thumbs-Down (two hands)

Begin

The children sit around the bunched-up chute. Walk around and put an "X" on their right hands and an "O" on their left hands. Have them grab the parachute using both hands with a Thumbs-Up grip. Then give rapid-fire commands changing the grips.

❋   *"Two hands, Thumbs-Down."*

❋   *"O (left) hand only. Thumbs-Down."*

❋   *"X (right) hand only, Thumbs-Up. Tap your head with your hand."*

❋   *"Two hands, Thumbs-Up."*

❋   *"O (left) hand only, Thumbs-Up. Wave to each other."*

❋   *"X (right) hand only, Thumbs-Down."*

Introduce the FLIP-FLOP

After they have finished the short warm-up exercise, have them put the parachute down. Until now they have moved the parachute by using a side-to-side jerking motion or a both arms up and both arms down motion. When they have done this individually, they have created a shallow waving movement. When they have gone up and down in unison, they have created giant waves.

Now the children are going to alternate arms — one arm up and one arm down. Have them grab the parachute with a Thumbs-Up grip. Start by having them slightly lift up their "X" (right) hand. Now bring the "X" (right) hand down and lift the "O" (left) hand. Continue this alternating motion. As they slowly FLIP-FLOP the chute, have them chant *"flip — flop"* as they alternate their arms. Continue at this slow speed until you think they have the rhythm of this new movement.

Now stand up, continue grabbing the parachute with the Thumbs-Up grip. Walk the parachute until it is fully spread out.

Now that it is fully spread out, slowly chant as you FLIP-FLOP the parachute. This will be slightly more tiring than when it was bunched-up, because you have the entire weight of the chute. Now let the children chant and flip-flop a little faster, a little faster, and then very fast. Bring them back to calm by reversing the order, a little slower, slower still, very slow. Remember to let your voice become quieter as the parachute slows down.

While resting, enjoy a fingerplay to get the wiggles out.

MY WIGGLES

I wiggle my fingers,
I wiggle my toes,
I wiggle my shoulders,
I wiggle my nose.
Now the wiggles are
  out of me,
And I'm just as still as
I can be.

Using the Thumbs-Down grip have them pick up the chute again. Say, *"Mary, wiggle your fingers at Jameel."* Continue giving children the opportunity to wiggle their fingers at each other.

WAVING

Have the children grab the parachute using the Thumbs-Down grip and stand up. Enjoy several waves at different speeds. Be sure to use the word *"STOP"* before you switch to another speed. Thus you might say, *"STOP. OK, let's wave a little faster."* Do that for awhile and say, *"STOP. This time let's wave real fast!"* When tired, say, *"STOP. Wave very slowly."* Now they are ready to listen to instruction and then enjoy the next activity.

Play BEACH BALL TOSS

In this game the children really need to listen to your commands. The first time the children play this game have them use the Thumbs-Up grip and keep the parachute around their waists. On other days, however, have them try the movements at their knees or over their heads.

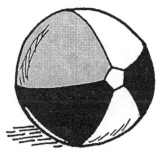

Toss the beach ball onto the chute. First have the children wave the parachute slowly. *"What is happening to the ball?"*

46

Continue the game by giving different directions, changing the motion and speed of the parachute.

- ❀ *"Flip-flop very slowly. STOP."*
- ❀ *"Wave very fast. STOP."*
- ❀ *"Jerk at a medium speed. STOP"*
- ❀ *"Slowly wave in unison. STOP."*
- ❀ *"Roll the ball around the chute. STOP."*
- ❀ And so on...

END

The last command should be *"Flip-flop slowly and walk the parachute back to the middle."* Take the beach ball off the chute. Have the children sit down. Talk about the three different movements.

- ❀ *"Which one was most tiring?"*
- ❀ *"Do they like to move the chute quickly or slowly?"*
- ❀ *"If they wanted the beach ball to go very fast, what movement and speed would they use?*
- ❀ *"Which movement is most relaxing?"*
- ❀ *"Did the beach ball ever fly off the parachute? What movement were you using?"*

After the discussion, have the children grab the bunched-up parachute with either the Thumbs-Up or Thumbs-Down grip, either one hand or two. Now go around the parachute, letting each child say what he is going to do next. After he has decided on his next activity, he should wiggle his thumbs or fingers and say, *"Good-bye"* as he transitions to his next activity.

SEVENTH SESSION

Objectives:
1. To review the different Parachute Positions.

2. To learn more Movements.

3. To introduce the Snap

Additional Equipment:
15-20 cotton balls
Popcorn popper, popcorn kernels, bowl, and salt

Body Position:
Standing

Hand Grip:
Thumbs-Up (two hands)

Begin

Grab the chute Thumbs-Up - Thumbs-Down and have the children move it to their different body parts as they slowly sing HEAD, SHOULDER, KNEES AND TOES After singing and moving several times, sit around the chute. Talk about all the different body parts they moved the chute to. Remind them that on other days they also moved the chute high over their heads as well as to their waists.

> **HEAD, SHOULDERS, KNEES, AND TOES**
>
> Head, shoulders, knees, and toes,
> Knees and toes, knees and toes,
>
> Head, shoulders, knees, and toes,
> Eyes, ears, nose, and mouth.

...Knees and toes...

48

Introduce the SNAP

Have everyone sit around the parachute and hold it with two hands using the Thumbs-Down grip. As with the waving motion, the snapping motion is both up - both down. Unlike the waving motion, the SNAP uses only your wrists, thus it is both wrists up - both wrists down. As you move your wrists, you also slightly pull back on the chute.

When you say, *"Snap"* have everyone quickly flick their wrists at the same time. Say, *"STOP."* Repeat the motion several times in a row — *"Snap - STOP, Snap - STOP, Snap - STOP."*

Play POPPING CORN

Have the children sit around the parachute. Talk about the entire process of making popcorn. Begin by gathering all of the ingredients, pouring in a little oil, and adding the kernels. What happens to the kernels as they cook? First you hear one or two go pop. Then several more and all of a sudden you hear all of them exploding in the popper. At this point teach the children the POPCORN SONG.

POPCORN SONG
(tune: Row, Row, Row Your Boat)

Pop, pop, pop your corn,
Pop it big and white.

Popping, popping, popping, popping,
Popping 'til its white.

As if on cue, the popping begins to subside. Soon you only hear one or two kernels. Finally, silence. Open the popper and the delicious white snack is almost ready. What is next? Of course, pour it in a bowl and add a little salt.

After discussing the popcorn making process, have the children pick up the parachute Thumbs-Down. Toss one cotton ball onto the parachute. Say, *"We're going to pretend that the cotton balls are the popcorn. First we hear only one or two kernels popping."* Using the snapping movement, begin to pop the popcorn. Gradually add all the balls. Change to a rapid flip-flop movement while all the kernels are popping. Return to the snapping movement as the popping subsides.

END

If the cotton balls have not flown off the chute, take them off. Have the children walk the parachute back to its bunched-up position.

Now everyone move to the snack area to make some real popcorn. While waiting for the popcorn to begin popping, enjoy several more popcorn rhymes.

EZ POPPER
by Dick Wilmes

Take a little oil.
Take a little seed.
Put them in a popper.
And heat is all you need.

THE POPCORN KERNEL
by Dick Wilmes

I am a popcorn kernel,
On the electric range,
With oil to my ankles,
Waiting for a change.

Pop, pop it's started happening, *(Flick fingers.)*
The noise has just begun.
Pop, pop there it goes again. *(Flick fingers.)*
It sounds like lots of fun.

Explosions to the left of me. *(Flick fingers.)*
Explosions to the right. *(Flick fingers.)*
I'm just about to blow my top,
I really think I might. *(Tap head)*

BANG!

51

EIGHTH SESSION

Objectives
1. To review the Four Parachute Movements.

2. To introduce going Under the Parachute

Additional Equipment:
Beach Ball

Body Position:
Standing

Hand Grip:
Thumbs-Down (two hands)

Begin

The children should sit around the bunched-up parachute. Tell them that today they are going to play several games under the parachute. Until now, they have done all of the activities grabbing onto the edge of the chute, moving in a variety of ways, and/or controlling a ball on top of the parachute.

Going under the chute is very exciting, but for some people also a little frightening, so as the children play, be very aware of feelings. It can also be very tiring, for as one or more children are under the chute, the others are usually holding it above their heads. Remember to provide enough resting opportunities.

While sitting, simply have the children grab a big handful of the parachute fabric Thumbs-Down, lift it above their heads, and duck under it. Now come out and lower the chute. *"What was it like under the chute?"* Now have them lift it again and duck under. This time turn to one of the people sitting next to them and say, *"Hi."*

Using the Thumbs-Down grip, have them stand and walk the parachute out.

Play BEACH BALL BOUNCE

When it is fully spread out, toss the beach ball onto the center of the parachute. Always using the Thumbs-Up grip, vary the movement, the speed, and the parachute position when giving commands:

* *"Hold the parachute over your head and wave it slowly. STOP."*
* *"Hold the parachute at your waist and snap it quickly one time. STOP."*
* *"Hold the parachute at your waist and wave it all together until it looms overhead. STOP. What happened to the ball?"*
* *"Hold the parachute at your knees and flip-flop it very fast. STOP."* (Remember to chant, *"flip-flop..."*)

Continue and then end with a slow relaxing command.

53

Play UNDER-THE-CHUTE GAMES

Now the children are ready to enjoy several under-the-chute activities. Remember to be aware of feelings and rest when necessary.

Play SHAKING HANDS

Have the group hold the parachute above their heads. You call out two children's names. They run under the chute to the center, shake hands and then run back to their places. Lower the chute. Ask the group, *"Who shook hands under the chute?"*

After they answer, have them raise the parachute again; you call out two more names. They run to the middle, shake hands and run back again. Lower the chute. Ask the children to name the four children who have shaken hands under the chute. Continue until everyone has had the opportunity to shake hands under the parachute.

Play MOVING

Have the children hold up the parachute. Call 2-3 children's names and tell them a movement. They do that movement around the inner edge of the chute. Each stops back at his place. Lower the chute; call on other children and name the movement they should do. Raise the chute and encourage them to move.

Possible Movements:

- ❋ Run
- ❋ Slide
- ❋ Gallop
- ❋ March
- ❋ Jog

- ❋ Hop
- ❋ Skip
- ❋ Tiptoe
- ❋ Crawl
- ❋ Leap

END

Have the children walk the chute to the middle. When they are there, have them remain standing. Play PEEK-A-BOO. Have everyone put their heads under the chute. When you say, *"Now"* they should quickly uncover their heads and say, *"Peek-a-boo"* to a person standing near them. Repeat several times.

After a while, have them lay the chute down and tiptoe to the next activity.

Warm-Up Exercises

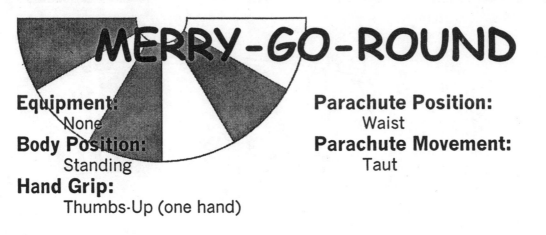

MERRY-GO-ROUND

Equipment:
None
Body Position:
Standing
Hand Grip:
Thumbs-Up (one hand)

Parachute Position:
Waist
Parachute Movement:
Taut

Activity

Have the children sit around the bunched up chute, and hold it Thumbs-Up. Sing the first verse of MERRY-GO-ROUND to learn the beat and activity.

Stand, hold the chute, and walk it out backwards.

When it is fully out, have all the children face to the right or left and hold the chute with one hand. Begin singing MERRY-GO-ROUND. As you sing, fly with the parachute.

Repeat the song, changing the movements each time. Have the last one be *"sit."* After everyone is sitting, take several deep breaths and relax.

> **MERRY-GO-ROUND**
> *(tune: Here We Go 'Round the Mulberry Bush)*
> by Liz Wilmes
>
> *Here we fly 'round the merry-go-round*
> *The merry-go-round, the merry-go-round.*
> *Here we fly 'round the merry-go-round.*
> *On a sunny (rainy, etc.) morning.*
>
> ❀ Slide
> ❀ Skate
> ❀ Hop
> ❀ Walk
> ❀ Jog

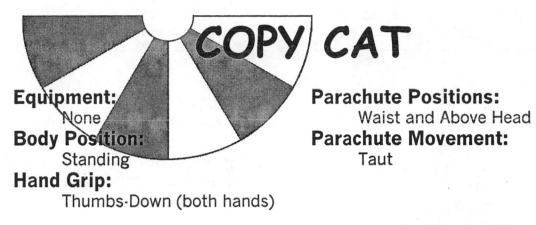

COPY CAT

Equipment:
None
Body Position:
Standing
Hand Grip:
Thumbs-Down (both hands)

Parachute Positions:
Waist and Above Head
Parachute Movement:
Taut

Activity

When all of the children are standing around the bunched-up chute, have them grab it using a Thumbs-Down grip. Have them think of an exercise that the group can do while holding onto the chute. Quickly go around the chute and have each child whisper his exercise to you. Walk the chute out.

Have the children hold the chute above their heads. One child goes under the chute, demonstrates his exercise, such as jumping up and down four times and runs back out. Lower the chute to waist high and everyone jump up and down four times, counting as you jump. Raise the chute for another child to demonstrate an exercise. Continue with several more childen.

59

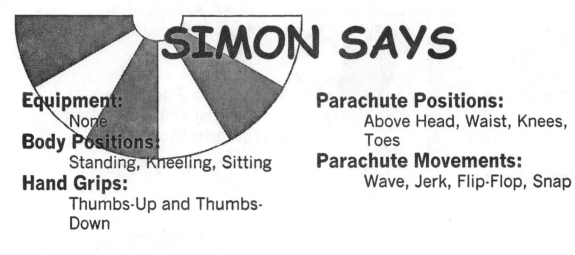

SIMON SAYS

Equipment:
None

Body Positions:
Standing, Kneeling, Sitting

Hand Grips:
Thumbs-Up and Thumbs-Down

Parachute Positions:
Above Head, Waist, Knees, Toes

Parachute Movements:
Wave, Jerk, Flip-Flop, Snap

Activity

As the children come to the bunched-up parachute, tell them to remain standing and grab the chute using the Thumbs-Up grip. Have them walk backwards until it is fully spread out. As they walk, encourage the children to gently wave the chute.

When the chute is fully out, play SIMON SAYS, concentrating on directions that use the four parachute movements, and the different parachute and body positions. Remember to say, *"Stop"* after you do each movement. This gives the children a chance to rest and listen to the next command from SIMON.

SIMON SAYS, "Wave the chute slowly. ------------ Stop"

SIMON SAYS, "Flip-flop the chute very fast." (Remember to chant "flip-flop" as you do this movement.) ------------ *"Stop."*

SIMON SAYS, "Sit down and stretch your legs under the chute. Wave the chute up as high as you can, creating a giant wave. Slowly bring it back down." ------------ *Stop."*

SIMON SAYS, "Stay sitting. Lift the chute over your head and wave to a friend. Bring the chute back down."

Continue with more directions.

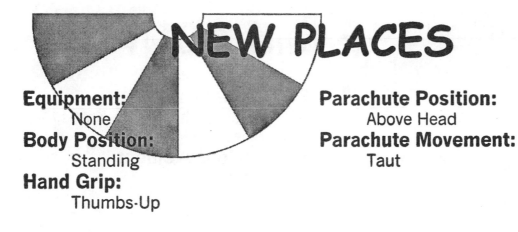

NEW PLACES

Equipment:
None
Body Position:
Standing
Hand Grip:
Thumbs-Up

Parachute Position:
Above Head
Parachute Movement:
Taut

Activity

Leaving the chute bunched up, have the children stand and hold hands, forming a wide circle around the chute. Move in a circle, doing several large body movements, such as sliding, galloping, taking giant steps, etc. Have the last movement bring the children close to the parachute so they can pull it out. You could say *"Tiptoe to the chute, hold it Thumbs-Up, and walk backwards until it is stretched out."*

Call out a child's name along with a movement, such as "twirl." Have the other children raise the chute above their heads. The child who was named, lets go of the chute and quickly "twirls" to a new place on the chute. After he has grabbed the chute in his new place, everyone lowers the chute. Call on another child, and continue playing.

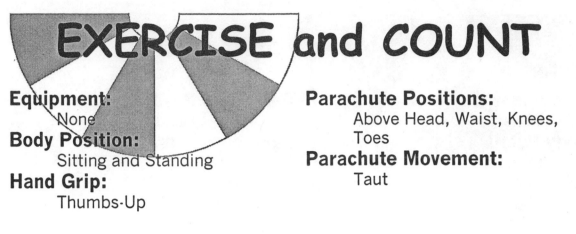

EXERCISE and COUNT

Equipment:
None
Body Position:
Sitting and Standing
Hand Grip:
Thumbs-Up

Parachute Positions:
Above Head, Waist, Knees, Toes
Parachute Movement:
Taut

Activity

As the children arrive at the bunched-up parachute, have them grab it Thumbs-Up and stretch their legs underneath. Scoot backwards until the chute is completely stretched out.

Leg Lifts – Have the children lift one leg, counting *"1, 2, 3"* as they lift and then lower the leg counting backwards, *"3, 2, 1."* Repeat with the other leg. Do several leg lifts.

Arm Stretches – Say, *"Hold the chute Thumbs-Down. Let's stretch our arms up in the air as high as we can."* Start counting as you lift the chute over your head. Count backwards as you lower the chute. Do several times.

Bend and Touch – Have the children sit with their legs stretched under the chute. Hold onto the chute, bend way over and touch their toes. Chant *"toes, toes, toes..."* as they reach. When they touch their toes, count *"1, 2, 3, 4, 5"* and sit back up. Call out another body part and continue.

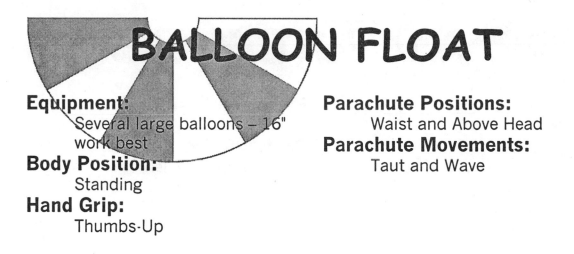

BALLOON FLOAT

Equipment:
Several large balloons – 16" work best

Body Position:
Standing

Hand Grip:
Thumbs-Up

Parachute Positions:
Waist and Above Head

Parachute Movements:
Taut and Wave

Activity

Have the children stand around the bunched-up chute and pick it up with a Thumbs-Up grip. Show the children one balloon. Ask them what color it is. Set the balloon on the chute. Have the children slowly walk backwards, keeping the balloon on the chute, until is completely stretched out.

Put several more balloons on the chute. Gently wave the chute. What are the balloons doing?

Have the children hold the parachute taut around their knees. You count *"1, 2, 3, up."* When you say *"up"* have the children quickly raise the chute as high as they can and then bring it down. Watch the balloons. *What are they doing now? Are they still on the chute? Are they floating in the air? How high are they? Are they moving fast? Slow?*

Have the children take a giant step towards the middle. Now the chute has a little slack. Count again *"1, 2, 3, up."* Have the children raise the chute again and bring it down. Now watch the balloons. *What's happening? Are they higher?*

Repeat the activity several more times, each time taking a giant step to the middle before lifting the chute. See if the children can get enough lift in the chute for the balloon/s to touch the ceiling before floating down. (This is a challenging but fun goal.)

PARACHUTE PULLS

Equipment:
　　None
Body Positions:
　　Standing, Kneeling, and
　　Sitting
Hand Grip:
　　Thumbs-Up

Parachute Positions:
　　Waist and Above Head
Parachute Movements:
　　Taut and Mushroom

Activity

When the children gather around the bunched-up chute, have them remain standing and grab it using the Thumbs-Up grip. Have the children slowly tighten their hold on the parachute, counting, *"1, 2, 3, 4, 5."* Pause and then slowly loosen their grip as they count backwards, *"5, 4, 3, 2, 1."* Relax. Repeat this several times.

Have the children turn around so their backs are to the chute. Hold onto the chute with both hands and walk the chute to its fully spread out position. Turn back around and face the

chute, holding it Thumbs-Up. Have the children hold the chute tightly, keep their feet flat on the floor, and lean back, pulling on the chute as they count, *"1, 2, 3, 4, 5."* Pause and straighten up as they count backwards, *"5, 4, 3, 2, 1."* Repeat this activity in a kneeling and sitting position. Which one was hardest?

Have the children turn their backs to the chute and hold onto the edge with a Thumbs-Down grip. Lean forward, counting, *"1, 2, 3, 4, 5."* Stand up straight, counting *"5, 4, 3, 2, 1*

1, 2, 3, 4, 5

64

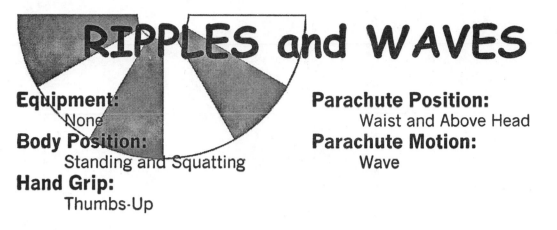

RIPPLES and WAVES

Equipment:
None

Body Position:
Standing and Squatting

Hand Grip:
Thumbs-Up

Parachute Position:
Waist and Above Head

Parachute Motion:
Wave

Activity

Grab the bunched-up chute with a Thumbs-Up grip. Slowly walk it out as you gently wave the chute.

Wave the chute in different ways to get a variety of movement.

Lazy Ripples – Gently move the chute up and down with short arm movements, between your waists and chests.

Rapid Ripples – Quickly move the chute up and down with short arm movements.

Large Waves – Slowly move the chute up and down with long arm movements, between your knees and head. Watch what happens to the chute. *Listen. Can you hear the waves?* (If you think your children are strong enough, do this a little faster. The waves become louder and fiercer.)

Tidal Waves – Have half the child squat and the other half stand. The half that is standing should hold the chute above their heads. When you say, *"The wave is coming!"* the children who are squatting, should slowly stand and the children who are standing should slowly squat. Repeat this movement several times. *Did you make a giant tidal wave?* (This is a difficult exercise. Make sure your children are strong enough. Stop if it is too challenging. Try it again in several months.)

Year 'Round Games

PARACHUTE "HELLO"

Themes:
Self-Concept
Friends

Body Position:
Sitting

Hand Grip:
Thumbs-Up

Parachute Position:
Waist/Overhead

Parachute Movement:
Taut

Equipment:
None

Warm-Up Exercise:
Simon Says, 60

Relaxing Activity:
Close Eyes and Pull, 129

Activity

Have the children stand up and hold the parachute. Lift it up high and everyone duck their heads under the chute and call out, *"Hello (friend's name)"* to a friend on the other side of the chute.

Lower the chute, and ask the children, *"What else do we say or do when we see a friend?"*

Using one of their suggestions, lift up the chute again and say *"hello"* to the friends who are next to you.

Think of several more ways to say *"hello"* and play again and again. Maybe the boys could say *"hello"* to each other, the girls, all those wearing a certain color, etc.

When finished, say the FRIENDS rhyme with the children. Talk about the different ways you thought of to say *"Hello."*

Extension: Play PARACHUTE "GOODBYE" near the end of the day.

FRIENDS

I say "Hello" to friends at school.
I'm happy as can be.
They are my special school friends.
I like them all, you see.

BALL BURP

Themes
Names
Any Time

Hand Grip:
Thumbs-Down

Parachute Position:
Waist
Chest

Parachute Movement:
Taut

Body Position:
Standing

Equipment:
Lots of sponge or yarn balls

Warm-Up Exercise:
Exercise and Count, 62

Relaxing Activity:
Breathe and Wave, 130

Activity

Have the children stand and hold the chute. Put the balls under the chute.

Name 2 children. All the others slowly raise the chute to their chest. The 2 children waddle into the middle and each tosses a ball up through the hole. The others give the chute a quick Snap and call out "BURP" as they see each ball. Lower the chute. Continue until all the balls have been "burped."

Extension: Toss balls in the air – catch them.

PEEK-A-BOO

Themes:
Self-Concept
Names

Hand Grip:
Thumbs-Down

Parachute Position:
Chest/Overhead

Parachute Movement:
Taut/Relaxed

Body Position:
Sitting

Equipment:
None

Warm-Up Exercise:
Simon, 60

Relaxing Activity:
Rock-A-Bye Baby, 127

Activity

Sit around the chute. Hold it Taut and scoot in a little.

Slowly say to the children, *"Peek-a-boo, I see ..."* As soon as the children hear you start to say, *"Peek-a-boo, I see"* they should quickly cover their heads with the chute. Look under the chute and call out the names of the first 3 or 4 children you see.

Have the children uncover their heads, take a deep breath, and play again and again.

Extension: Play HIDE 'N SEEK outside.

ZOO PARADE

Themes:
Zoo
Animals

Body Position:
Standing

Hand Grip:
Thumbs-Up

Parachute Position:
Waist and Overhead

Parachute Movement:
Taut

Equipment:
Hula-Hoop

Warm-Up Exercise:
Simon Says, 60

Relaxing Activity:
Rock-A-Bye Baby, 127
(with a bear)

Activity

Sit around the chute and say ZOO PARADE with the children. Have the children call out different zoo animals they remember.

ZOO PARADE

by Dick Wilmes

Come and join the big parade.
It starts with you and me.
We'll march around the city zoo
And see who we can see.

Ooh ooh ee ee AH AH!

Stand and name 2 children. Everyone else lift the chute over their heads. (Put the hula-hoop in the middle.) The children go under the chute, stand inside the hula-hoop, and pretend to be zoo animals. Everyone calls out the names of the animals.

The children go back to their place. Lower the chute. Name another pair of children and continue playing.

Extension: Read SAM WHO NEVER FORGETS by Eve Rice.

HOKEY-POKEY

Themes:
Body Awareness
Any Time

Body Position:
Standing

Hand Grip:
Thumbs-Up

Parachute Position:
Waist/Overhead

Parachute Movement:
Jerk

Equipment:
None

Warm-Up Exercise:
Simon Says, 60

Relaxing Activity:
Rag Doll, 128

Activity

Stand around the chute. Take one giant step to the middle so there is slack in the chute.

Start singing the HOKEY-POKEY and doing the appropriate motions while hanging onto the chute. When you sing, *"You do the hokey-pokey and turn yourself around, that's what's all about,"* raise the chute and Jerk it several times. Girls let go of the chute and quickly turn around. As the girls come back, they grab the chute. When everyone is ready, sing the next verse. Boys are next. Keep singing

Hint: This is challenging in the beginning, but lots of fun.

Extension: Sing HOKEY-POKEY while waiting for children to gather.

71

HAPPY BIRTHDAY

Themes:
Birthdays
Self-Concept
Numbers

Body Position:
Standing

Hand Grip:
Thumbs-Down

Parachute Position:
Waist

Parachute Movement:
Snap

Equipment:
None

Warm-Up Exercise:
Ripples and Waves, 65

Relaxing Activity:
Good-Bye Balloons, 128
(*Number of balloons the child is old*)

Happy Birthday to you

FOUR!

Activities

Child's Birthday – Put balloons on the parachute. Sing HAPPY BIRTHDAY to the birthday child as you gently Wave the parachute.

Everyone's Birthday – Call on a child. That child tells the others his real age or an age he would like to be. The children Snap the chute the appropriate number of times, counting aloud as they Snap. Look at the child and call out, *"Happy birthday, Greg!"* Ask another child how old she is today. Continue until everyone has celebrated a birthday.

Extension: Hang the balloons from your ceiling.

BEANBAG SHUTTLE

Themes:
Colors
Friends
Any Time

Body Position:
Standing

Hand Grip:
Thumbs-Down

Parachute Position:
Waist/Overhead

Parachute Movement:
Taut/Relaxed

Equipment:
Beanbags
(one per child)

Warm-Up Exercise:
New Places, 61

Relaxing Activity:
SHHH!, 126

Activity

Put the beanbags under the chute. Have the children count, *"1, 2, 3, 4, 5"* as they lift up the chute.

Name 2 children. Have them run under the chute and each grab a beanbag. Take their beanbags to 2 other children and lay them next to those children's feet. Run back to their places on the chute.

As they're running, the other children lower the chute and count, *"5, 4, 3, 2, 1."* Play until all the beanbags have been SHUTTLED.

Extension: Toss beanbags in a pail.

FLOAT YOUR CHUTE

Themes:
Sky
Weather

Body Position:
Standing

Hand Grip:
Thumbs-Down

Parachute Position:
Overhead

Parachute Movement:
Taut

Equipment:
None

Warm-Up Exercise:
Parachute Pulls, 64

Relaxing Activity:
Breathe, 130

Activity

Hold the parachute overhead with both hands. Run in one direction.

After the children have run about halfway around, call out, *"Let go!"* Watch the chute float to the ground.

Pick up the chute, play again running in the opposite direction.

Extension: Find shapes in big, billowy clouds.

BUILD A TOWER

Themes:
Homes
Community

Body Position:
Kneeling/Standing

Hand Grip:
Thumbs-Up

Parachute Position:
Waist/Overhead

Parachute Movement:
Taut

Equipment:
Cardboard Blocks

Warm-Up Exercise:
New Places, 61

Relaxing Activity:
SHHH!, 126

Activity

Put the large blocks under the chute. The children kneel around the chute. Name 2 children. Raise the chute as you all chant, *"Up-up-up-up."* The 2 children crawl under the chute and stack 2 blocks to begin making a tower. Crawl back.

Lower the chute chanting, *"Down-down-down-down."* Name 2 more children. Raise the chute and chant.

Those 2 children crawl to the tower and add 2 more blocks.

Continue until the tower gets too tall. Have the children stand. Continue building. (If it falls over, just rebuild it.) After the tower is complete, take it down 2 blocks at a time.

Extension: Encourage more tower building in the block area.

PASS THE CHUTE

Themes:
Cooperation
Friendship

Body Position:
Kneeling

Hand Grip:
Thumbs-Up

Parachute Position:
Waist

Parachute Movement:
Taut

Equipment:
None

Warm-Up Exercise:
Parachute Pulls, 61

Relaxing Exercise:
Breathe and Wave, 130

Activity

Have the children kneel around the chute. Teach them the PASS THE CHUTE song. Pick up the chute. Begin to slowly sing while slowly passing the chute to each other. Shout out the word, "STOP." Everyone "freeze" the chute.

Start singing at a different speed. Pass the chute at the speed you're singing. Play several more times at even different speeds. Another time go in the reverse order.

Extension: When you're eating snack and lunch, pass the food and drinks to each other.

> **PASS THE CHUTE**
> (tune: Row, Row, Row Your Boat)
>
> *Pass, pass, pass the chute*
> *Pass it round and round.*
>
> *Passing, passing, passing, passing,*
> *Passing 'til it STOPS!*

BEANBAG BUCKET

Themes:
Colors
Numbers

Body Position:
Kneeling

Hand Grip:
Thumbs-Up

Parachute Position:
Waist

Parachute Movement:
Flip-Flop

Equipment:
Beanbags
Pail

Warm-Up Exercise:
Exercise and Count, 62

Relaxing Activity:
Gunk, Gunk, 125

Activity

Put the bucket and the beanbags under the parachute.

Name several children. Tell each one what color beanbag to look for. Everyone lift the chute. The children quickly go under the chute, find their color beanbag, and put it in the bucket. Lower the chute. Continue with other children

Extension: Make a giant square on your floor with colored tape. Slide the beanbags into it.

NAME EXCHANGE

Themes:
Names
Self-Concept
Any Time

Body Position:
Standing

Hand Grip:
Thumbs-Up

Parachute Position:
Waist/Overhead

Parachute Movement:
Jerk

Equipment:
None

Warm-Up Exercise:
Merry-Go-Round, 58

Relaxing Activity:
See a Lassie?, 126

Activity

Eric and Jamie!

Name 2 children. Others raise the chute overhead and Jerk it side to side. The 2 children run to the middle, give each other a hug or high-5, and run to their friend's place on the chute. Lower the chute.

Play again and again, always mixing up the names.

Extension: Play NAME EXCHANGE without the parachute.

WIGGLING WORMS

By: Jane Flynn

Themes
Worms
Spring

Body Position:
Kneeling

Hand Grip:
Thumbs-Up

Parachute Position:
Waist

Parachute Movement:
Jerk

Equipment:
None

Warm-Up Exercise:
New Places, 61

Relaxing Activity:
Gunk, Gunk Went the
Little Green Frog, 125

Activity

Divide the children into 2 groups. Have one group kneel around the chute, pick it up to chest height, and Wave it gently. Tell the other group to lie on their tummies, wiggle under the chute and pretend they are worms wiggling under the ground.

While one group is wiggling like worms, everyone else sing the WIGGLING WORMS. As they sing, Wave the chute. (high and low, fast and slow, etc.)

After several verses, start singing the last verse. Change groups. Let the worms wiggle out and grab the chute while the new worms are wiggling under.

Extension: Look for worms on the playground. Be careful not to step on them.

WIGGLING WORMS
(tune: Farmer In the Dell)

The worms are wiggling slow,
The worms are wiggling slow,
Hi ho the derri-o,
The worms are wiggling slow.

The worms are wiggling fast...
The worms are wiggling backwards...
The worms are wiggling sideways...
The worms are rolling over...

Last command:
The worms are wiggling out...
The worms are wiggling out...
Hi, ho the derri-o
The worms are wiggling out.

77

FLY YOUR KITE

Themes:
Self Concept
Any Time

Body Position:
Standing

Hand Grip:
Thumbs-Down

Parachute Position:
Overhead

Parachute Movement:
Relaxed

Equipment:
None

Warm-Up Exercise:
Exercise and Count, 62

Relaxing Activity:
Close Eyes and Pull, 129

Activity

Fold the parachute in half. Have 7-8 children hold the chute along the unfolded edge with one hand. The rest slowly sing FLY YOUR KITE.

The children holding the parachute should slowly jog in one direction. As they gain a little more speed, they should raise their arms higher and higher. This will help lift the chute and let it fly like a kite. After the children have sung FLY YOUR KITE several times, switch groups and play again.

Once the children can control their new kite, have them Wave it by slowly raising and lowering their arms as they jog.

> ### FLY YOUR KITE
> (tune: Row, Row, Row Your Boat)
>
> by Dick Wilmes
>
> *Fly, fly, fly your kite.*
> *Fly it up and down.*
>
> *Flying, flying, flying, flying*
> *Flying all around.*

Extension: Give each child a plastic grocery bag. Hang onto the handles and run! So much fun!

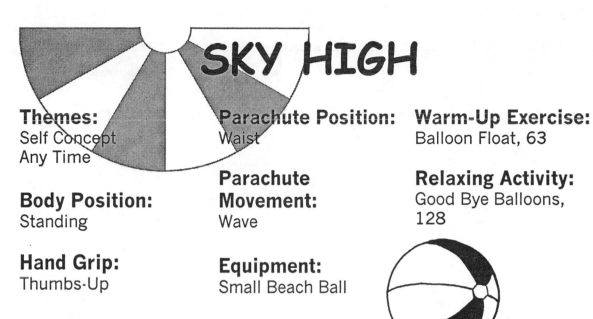

SKY HIGH

Themes:
Self Concept
Any Time

Body Position:
Standing

Hand Grip:
Thumbs-Up

Parachute Position:
Waist

Parachute Movement:
Wave

Equipment:
Small Beach Ball

Warm-Up Exercise:
Balloon Float, 63

Relaxing Activity:
Good Bye Balloons, 128

Activity

Stand around the chute. Put the beach ball in the middle.

All together Wave the chute once – STOP. Take a step into the middle. Wave the chute a little higher. STOP. *"Did the beach ball lift off the chute?"* Take another step in. Wave the chute higher and harder. *"Did the ball go higher?"* Keep playing – the sky is the limit.

Extension: Toss balls in the air and catch them.

TUG-A-CHUTE "FREEZE"

Themes:
Self Concept
Body Awareness

Body Position:
Sit/Kneel/Stand

Hand Grip:
Thumbs-Up

Parachute Position:
Waist

Parachute Movement:
Pulling

Equipment:
None

Warm-Up Exercise:
Parachute Pulls, 64

Relaxing Activity:
Roll Up, 131

Activity

Divide the children into 2 groups. Have them sit opposite each other on 2 sides of the parachute. Name the groups, Side 1 and Side 2. Tell them that when you say *"Go,"* Side 1 should tug on the chute, pulling the children on Side 2 forward. Then Side 2 should tug on the chute, pulling the children on Side 1 forward. Continue this back and forth motion until the children get the rhythm.

Now play TUG-A-CHUTE "FREEZE." Have Side 1 start tugging. Count as the children tug back and forth. Without indication, say *"Freeze!"* Everyone stop! Have the children rest a minute and take a deep breath. Say, *"Go."* Start counting as the children tug back and forth. *"Freeze"* again. Continue in this way, always counting to a different number before saying, *"Freeze."*

Extension: Tie several scarves to your fence. Encourage the children to pull on the scarves, count to 3, and relax.

TUMMY TAG

Themes:
Body Awareness
Summer
Any Time

Body Position:
Kneeling

Hand Grip:
Thumbs-Up

Parachute Position:
Shoulder

Parachute Movement:
Flip-Flop

Equipment:
None

Warm-Up Exercise:
New Places, 61

Relaxing Activity:
SHHH!, 126

Activity

Have the children kneel and hold the chute a few feet off the ground. Name several children. Have them lie on their stomachs and "crawl" under the chute. Name one more child. He is "it." He lies on his stomach at the edge of the chute.

When you say, *"Go,"* the child who is "it" begins chasing the others. When a child is tagged, he becomes "it" also. Now the 2 children chase the others. Play until everyone has been tagged. Play again with other children.

Extension: Play regular tag outside.

81

POP FLIES

Themes:
Spring/Summer
Sports

Body Position:
Standing

Hand Grip:
Thumbs-Up

Parachute Position:
Waist

Parachute Movement:
Wave

Equipment:
Small Beach Ball

Warm-Up Exercises:
Balloon Float, 63

Relaxing Activities:
Balloon Goodbye, 128

Activity

Everyone stand, holding the chute. Name one child to let go of the chute and move 3 or 4 giant steps away. Put the ball on the chute. Have the children slowly Wave the chute. After several waves everyone say, *"1, 2, 3 Toss!"*

As the group says *"Toss,"* the children nearest the beach ball gives the chute a hard upward Wave, so the ball flies off the chute towards the catcher. The child standing off the chute catches the ball, tosses it back onto the chute, and takes his place again on the chute.

Another child should drop off the chute to catch the ball. Continue until all the children have had a chance to be the catcher. The last person puts the ball away.

Extension: Play CATCH outside.

WINDOW WASHERS

Themes:
Community Helpers
Water
Numbers

Body Position:
Standing

Hand Grip:
Thumbs-Down

Parachute Position:
All

Parachute Movement:
Jerk

Equipment:
None

Warm-Up Exercises:
New Places, 61

Relaxing Activity:
Did You Ever See a Lassie, 126

Activity

Have the children stand around the parachute and pretend they are window washers. They are going to be very busy washing the windows on a 10 story building.

Have the window washers bend down and grab the chute, getting ready to wash the ground floor windows. Jerk the chute back and forth as if washing the windows. As the children are washing, have them chant *"swish, swish, swish."* Raise the chute slightly. Call out *"Second floor."* Wash these windows — *"swish, swish, swish."* Go up to the third level and continue until the windows on all 10 floors have been washed.

ALL DONE! Have the window washers slowly come back down to the ground floor. Count *"10 - 9 - 8 - 7 - 6 - 5 - 4 - 3 - 2 - 1"* as you go. Sit and relax after a big job.

Extension: Wash the trikes outside.

Swish, swish, swish...

SIMON SAYS

Themes:
Self Concept

Body Position:
Standing

Hand Grip:
Thumbs-Down

Parachute Position:
All

Parachute Movement:
All

Equipment:
Beach Ball

Warm-Up Exercise:
Ballon Float, 62

Relaxing Activity:
Breathe and Wave, 130

Activity

Toss the beach ball on the parachute. Say to the children, *"Listen carefully as Simon tells you what to do with the beach ball."*

SIMON SAYS, *"Roll the beach ball around the edge of the chute."*

SIMON SAYS, *"Snap the chute 5 times. Count as you snap."*

Continue

Extension: Take several beach balls outside. Play SIMON SAYS again.

PARACHUTE ROLLER BALL

Themes:
Friends
Numbers

Body Position:
Standing

Hand Grip:
Thumbs-Up

Parachute Position:
Waist

Parachute Movement:
Wave

Equipment:
Sponge ball

Warm-Up Exercise:
Ripples/Waves, 65

Relaxing Activity:
Are You Sleeping?, 131

Activity

Roll the sponge ball back and forth across the parachute. Go as fast as you can. Count as you roll. How many times did you roll it back and forth? Write the number on your score sheet.

Play again and record that number. Continue on different days, always keeping score. What's your highest score? Lowest score? How many times have you played?

Extension: Play catch with a friend. Count how many times you catch it. Play again and again.

RING AROUND the ROSIE

Themes:
Nursery Rhymes
Any Time

Body Position:
Standing

Hand Grip:
Thumbs-Up

Parachute Position:
Waist

Parachute Movement:
Wave

Equipment:
None

Warm-Up Exercise:
Merry-Go-Round, 58

Relaxing Activity:
Are You Sleeping?, 131

Activity

Everyone hold the parachute with one hand. Jog around in a circle as you sing the first verse of RING AROUND THE ROSIE. Fall down.

Everyone lie down and quietly sing the second verse. Jump up and play again.

Extension: Play RING AROUND THE ROSIE outside with small and large groups of children.

RING AROUND THE ROSIE

Ring around the rosie.
Pocketful of posie.
Ashes, ashes
We all fall down.

Cows in the meadow
Lying down and sleeping.
Thunder, lightening
We all stand up!

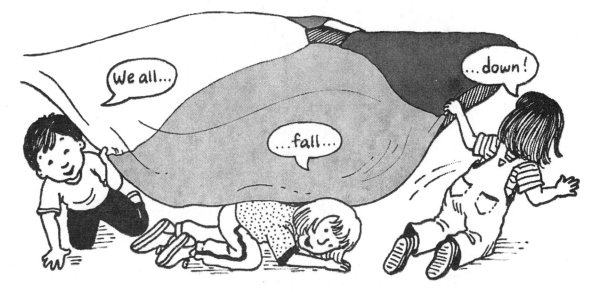

NAME YOUR BODY PARTS

Themes:
Body Awareness
Self Concept

Body Position:
Sitting

Hand Grip:
Thumbs-Up

Parachute Position:
Waist

Parachute Movement:
Taut

Equipment:
None

Warm-Up Exercise:
Simon Says, 60

Relaxing Activity:
Rag Doll, 128

Activity

Have all the children sit around the chute and raise it slightly off the ground. Have everyone close their eyes. Walk around the chute and tap a child on the shoulder. She should crawl under the chute to the middle.

Have her poke a part of her body (elbow, arm, foot, knee, finger, etc.) through the hole. Say to the other children, *"Open your eyes. What body part do you see peeking through the hole in our parachute?"*

Everyone opens their eyes and looks at the middle of the chute and calls out the body part they see. The child under the chute crawls out and sits back at her place on the chute. Now everyone's ready to play again.

Leg!

Extension:
Trace children's bodies on butcher paper. Let them color and collage them. Hang in the hall.

PARACHUTE GOLF

Themes:
Spring/Summer
Numbers

Body Position:
Standing

Hand Grip:
Thumbs-Dow

Parachute Position:
Waist

Parachute Movement:
Wave

Equipment:
Sponge Ball
Scorecard

Warm-Up Exercise:
Balloon Float, 63

Relaxing Activity:
Good-Bye Balloons,
128

Activity

	1	2	3	4	5	6	7	8	9
1	3	4	2	5					
2									
3									
4									
5									

Before the children can go to the golf course they must practice on the putting green. Toss the ball on the chute. Begin Waving the chute, trying to maneuver the ball through the hole. When the ball is sunk, name someone to go under the chute, get the ball, and toss it back on the chute.

After the children have had enough practice, show them the scorecard. Tell them that now they are going to count how many "strokes" it takes them to get the ball in the hole. Have the children count aloud as they Wave the chute.

After the children sink the ball, write the number of strokes on the scorecard. Continue in this manner with all 9 holes.

Extension: Using plastic golf clubs and soft balls, play "miniature golf" outside.

LISTEN TO THE BEAT

Themes:
Musical Instruments
Parades
Any Time

Body Position:
Standing

Hand Grip:
Thumbs-Up

Parachute Position:
Waist

Parachute Movement:
Taut

Equipment:
Drum

Warm-Up Exercise:
Merry-Go-Round, 58

Relaxing Activity:
Roll Up, 131

Activity

Have an adult stand near the parachute with the drum. Have the children stand around the parachute, holding it with 2 hands.

Beat the drum slowly. Encourage the children to slowly march in place. STOP beating. The children stop marching. Beat the drum at a different speed. The children march in place to the new beat.

Now have the children face in one direction and hold the chute with one hand. Start beating the drum. Have the children march in a circle as you beat. STOP!
Continue with a new beat:
* Fast for a short time.
* Walking pace for a long time.
* Slow for a short time.
* And so on.

At the end, have the children hold the chute with 2 hands. Beat the drum very slowly as the children march in place in slo-o-o-w motion.

Extension: Put out several drums for the children to use. Encourage them to parade around the room.

SINK THE "RED BALL"

Themes:
Colors
Friends

Parachute Position:
Waist

Warm-Up Exercise:
Ripples and Waves, 65

Body Position:
Standing

Parachute Movement:
Wave

Relaxing Activity:
Did You Ever See A
    Lassie?, 126

Hand Grip:
Thumbs-Up

Equipment:
2 Different Colored
    Yarn Balls

Activity

Put both yarn balls on the chute. Call out one color. Have the children work together to sink that ball down the hole.

After that ball has been sunk, call out the color of the second ball. Sink it. (If by chance you sink the wrong ball, just ask a child to get it and toss back on the chute.)

Extension: Have a bucket of colored yarn balls. Sit on the floor in small groups and roll 3-4 balls back and forth at one time.

SNAP BALL

Themes:
Numbers
Any Time

Body Position:
Kneel/Stand

Hand Grip:
Thumbs-Down

Parachute Position:
Waist

Parachute Movement:
Snap

Equipment:
Small Beach Ball

Warm-Up Exercise:
Exercise and Count, 62

Relaxing Activity:
Wave and Sing, 124

Activity

Toss the beach ball in the middle of the chute. Say to the children, *"Hold on tight! Let's Snap the chute one time and see how high the ball jumps."* (Do it.) *"Let's Snap harder and see if we can make the ball jump higher."* (Do it.)

Try Other Ball Challenges

* Start with the ball on one side of the chute. Snap the chute several times, trying to move the ball to the other side.

* Call out a number. Snap the chute rapidly that many times.

* Play NUMBER ROCK, on the album We All Live Together, Volume 2 by Greg and Steve. Snap the chute as you count with the song.

BUG IN MY CHUTE

Themes:
Self Concept
Bugs and Insects

Body Position:
Sitting

Hand Grip:
Thumbs-Up

Parachute Position:
Waist

Parachute Movement:
Taut

Equipment:
None

Warm-Up Exercise:
Copy Cat, 59

Relaxing Activity:
Roll-Up, 131

Activity

Have the children sit around the chute. Say the BUG IN MY CHUTE rhyme several times.

BUG IN MY CHUTE

Bug in my chute
Bug in my chute
Who is that bug in my chute?

Once the children are familiar with the rhyme, have them hold the chute up a little bit and close their eyes. While the children's eyes are closed, walk around the chute. Tap a child on the shoulder. She should crawl under the chute.

Have the children open their eyes and say BUG IN MY CHUTE. As they are saying the rhyme, have them look around and figure out who is missing. When someone thinks he knows, have him call out the child's name.

If the child is right, have the child under the chute wave her hand through the hole and then crawl out. If not, just stay under the chute and let the children keep guessing.

Extension: Look for bugs on your neighborhood walks.

Sam!

91

GIANT TOOTSIE ROLL

Themes:
Self-Concept
Friends

Body Position:
Standing

Hand Grip:
Thumbs-Up

Parachute Position:
Waist

Parachute Movement:
Taut

Equipment:
None

Warm-Up:
Parachute Pulls, 64

Relaxing Activity:
Close Your Eyes and
    Pull, 129

Activity

Divide the children in 2 equal groups. Have one group kneel on one side of the chute and the other group kneel on the opposite side.

Say to one group, *"I want you to hold the parachute really tight, while your friends are rolling up their side into a GIANT TOOTSIE ROLL."*

tootsie roll...

(Do it. As the children are rolling up the chute, have everyone chant, *"tootsie roll, tootsie roll, ..."* Stop when you get to the middle.) Now have the first group hold onto their half of the tootsie roll. The second group rolls up their side of the chute. Everyone chants, *"tootsie roll..."* as the second group rolls.

After both groups have made their tootsie rolls, have each group, one at a time, unroll their ROLLS.

Extension: Make ROLL-UP SANDWICHES. Let the children use rolling pins to flatten pieces of bread. Spread peanut butter or spreadable cheese on each piece and then roll them up! Eat and enjoy.

FLOATING CLOUDS

Themes:
Sky
Any Time

Body Position:
Standing

Hand Grip:
Thumbs-Up

Parachute Position:
Waist

Parachute Movement:
Giant Wave

Equipment:
13 gallon white trash bag ("Blow" up. Use a twist-um to tie shut. Presto a giant cloud!)

Warm-Up:
Balloon Float, 63

Relaxing Activity:
This Old Man, 130

Activity

Have the children stand around the parachute and hold it with a Thumbs-Up grip. Take one step into the middle so the parachute has a little slack. Toss the "cloud" onto the parachute.

All together have the children give the parachute a Giant Wave. Watch the cloud. When it floats back to the chute, give another Giant Wave. Did the cloud float higher this time? (Hint: The cloud moves very slowly and quietly. It is a wonderful sensory experience.)

Now the children have a sense for how their cloud floats. Roll it to one side of the chute. Have the children on that side give the cloud a Giant Wave so it floats to the other side of the chute. (Hint: The children may need to give the chute several Giant Waves while the others lower their side of the chute.) The children on the second side catch the floating cloud and give it a Giant Wave back. Continue FLOATING THE CLOUD between the two sides of the chute.

Play Again: Put several "clouds" on the chute. Wave them high above you. You'll love the quiet sensation. Take the "giant clouds" outside and play.

Holiday and
Seasonal
Games

HAPPY NEW YEAR!

Themes:
New Years Day
Numbers
Any Celebration

Body Position:
Stand

Hand Grip:
Thumbs-Up

Parachute Position:
Waist/Overhead

Parachute Movement:
Snap, Wave

Equipment:
Balloons

Warm-Up Exercise:
Exercise and Count, 62

Relaxing Activity:
Good-Bye Balloons, 128

Happy New Year!

Activity

Sit around the parachute and slowly count backwards from 10 to 1. After the children say *"1,"* everyone shout, *"Happy New Year!"*

Now stand and hold the parachute. Slowly count backwards – *"10, 9, 8, 7, 6, 5, 4, 3, 2, 1."* As the children say each number have them give the chute a Giant Snap. After they say *"1,"* have them Wave the chute into a giant mushroom shape and shout *"Happy New Year!"*

Put several colorful balloons on the chute. Slowly count backwards and Snap the chute as you did before. Watch the balloons jump around the chute. At the end, Wave the chute as high as you can and shout *"Happy New Year!"* How high did the balloons go? Watch them slowly float back down. Whisper *"Happy New Year."*

Extension: Do this activity on children's birthdays. Instead of counting to 10, count the age of the birthday child.

PARACHUTE BLIZZARD

By: Jane Flynn

Themes:
Winter
Snow
Weather

Body Position:
Stand

Hand Grip:
Thumbs-Up

Parachute Position:
Waist

Parachute Movement:
Wave or Flip-Flop

Equipment:
Styrofoam Packing
    Pieces and/or Small
    White Pom-Poms

Warm-Up Exercise:
Ripples and Waves, 65

Relaxing Activity:
Breathe and Wave, 130

Activity

Have the children stand and hold the parachute. Add a few pieces of "snow" (styrofoam/pompoms). Quickly Wave the parachute up in the air, so the pieces fly like snow flurries. Say to the children, *"Look! It's starting to snow."*

Add a few more pieces. Wave the chute again. *"Oh, it's snowing even more!"* Add more and more "snow." Say, *"Can you believe, it's snowing even harder!"* Keep adding "snow." Wave the chute even higher and faster until it looks like a blizzard. (The "snow" will probably fly off the chute. That's OK.)

After the blizzard has stopped, lay the chute down.

Pair off the children, giving each pair a bag. Have them fill their bags with "snow" and give them to you for future blizzards.

Extension: Watch the snow fall. If temperature permits, go outside and feel the snow on your face. Listen to it come down. Is it noisy?

97

SHADOWS

Themes:
Winter
Snow
Weather

Body Position:
Stand

Hand Grip:
Thumbs-Up

Parachute Position:
Waist

Parachute Movement:
Wave

Equipment:
Large Flashlight Held by a Child or an Adult

Warm-Up Exercise:
Ripples and Waves, 65

Relaxing Activity:
Breathe and Wave, 130

Activity

Have the children pretend they are ground hogs hibernating in their holes, by lying on the floor under the edge of the chute. As they are hibernating, tell them the legend of how the ground hog looks for his shadow. (Have someone stand near the wall and hold the flashlight.)

As you tell how the ground hog comes out of his burrow to look for his shadow, tap several children on the shoulders to come out and look for their shadows. They should move like ground hogs over to the "sun" (flashlight), discover their shadows, and run back to their hole. Continue tapping the "ground hogs" and letting them look for their shadow.

End the story by saying, *"It looks like all the ground hogs saw their shadows today. There will be 6 more weeks of cold winter weather. Let's count to 6."* (Everyone count.)

Extension: Hang a white sheet on the wall. Attach a spotlight to the ceiling and shine it on the sheet. Encourage the children to make hand, finger, and body shadows on the sheet.

"HEARTEE" TIME

Themes:
Self-Concept
Alphabet

Body Position:
Stand

Hand Grip:
Thumbs-Up

Parachute Position:
Waist

Parachute Movement:
Wave

Equipment:
Heart-Shaped Name
Card for Each Child

Warm-Up Exercise:
Ripples and Waves, 65

Relaxing Activity:
Breathe and Wave, 130

Activity

Teach the children the WHAT DO YOU SAY chant. After the children know the chant, stand and lift the chute over their heads. Have several children put the heart shaped name cards, face-up, under the chute.

WHAT DO YOU SAY?

"Eric, Eric (change name each time) *what do you say!*
Skate (change movement each time) *around the chute today."*

Lower the chute. Name 2 or 3 children and a movement. Everyone else raise the chute. The children you named go under the chute doing the movement, as they look for their hearts. Everyone else chants.

After each child finds his heart, he picks it up and does the movement back to his place.

Continue until everyone has his heart.

Extension: Decorate the hearts with red, white, and pink collage materials.

99

THUNDERSTORM

By: Jane Flynn

Themes:
Spring
Rain
Weather

Body Position:
Sit or Stand

Hand Grip:
Thumbs-Up

Parachute Position:
Waist

Parachute Movement:
Flip-Flip

Equipment:
Several Tennis Balls

Warm-Up Exercise:
Parachute Pulls, 64

Relaxing Activity:
Wave and Sing, 124

Activity

Have the children sit or stand around the parachute. Toss the tennis balls on it. Tell the children that today they are going to pretend that their parachute is a huge ocean and the tennis balls are ships, sailing across the water. Have the children slowly roll the balls back and forth across the chute. (Remember, tennis balls move quickly. You only need to tip the chute slowly.)

After the children have "sailed their ships" back and forth across the ocean several times, begin the story: (See Next Page)

Extension: Talk with children about wind, thunder, and lightening.

THUNDERSTORM

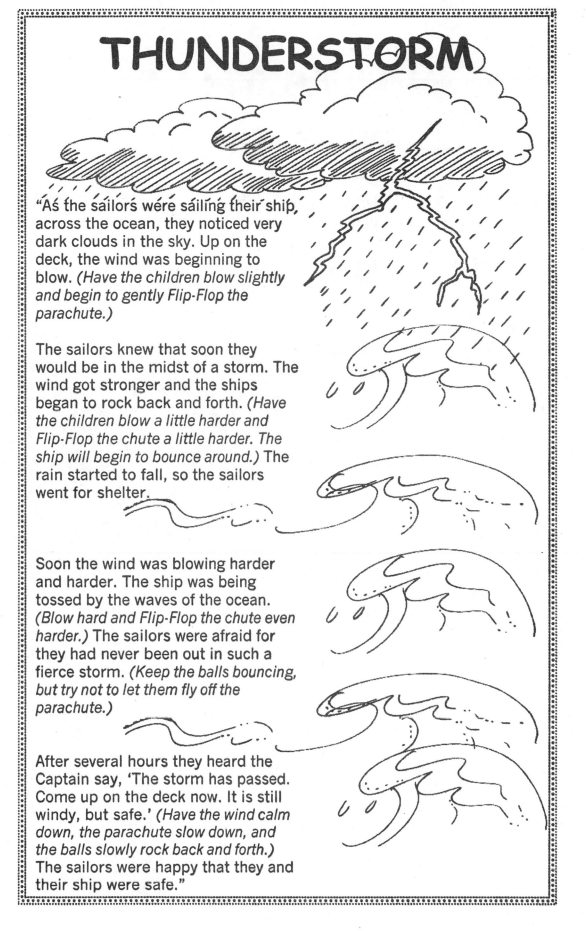

"As the sailors were sailing their ship, across the ocean, they noticed very dark clouds in the sky. Up on the deck, the wind was beginning to blow. *(Have the children blow slightly and begin to gently Flip-Flop the parachute.)*

The sailors knew that soon they would be in the midst of a storm. The wind got stronger and the ships began to rock back and forth. *(Have the children blow a little harder and Flip-Flop the chute a little harder. The ship will begin to bounce around.)* The rain started to fall, so the sailors went for shelter.

Soon the wind was blowing harder and harder. The ship was being tossed by the waves of the ocean. *(Blow hard and Flip-Flop the chute even harder.)* The sailors were afraid for they had never been out in such a fierce storm. *(Keep the balls bouncing, but try not to let them fly off the parachute.)*

After several hours they heard the Captain say, 'The storm has passed. Come up on the deck now. It is still windy, but safe.' *(Have the wind calm down, the parachute slow down, and the balls slowly rock back and forth.)* The sailors were happy that they and their ship were safe."

WHO'S THAT LEPRECHAUN?

Themes:
St. Patrick's Day

Body Position:
Stand

Hand Grip:
Thumbs-Up

Parachute Position:
Waist/Overhead

Parachute Movement:
Passing

Equipment:
3 or 4 Green Hats

Warm-Up Exercise:
Exercise and count, 62

Relaxing Activity:
Gunk, Gunk, 125

Activity

Have the children stand around the chute. Put the green hats around the chute edge.

At a regular pace, start passing the chute, chanting, *"Pass, pass, pass, pass, STOP"* etc. The children who have the green hats in front of them, should put them on. The others raise the chute. Say, *"All the "leprechauns," hop to another leprechaun's place."* The children with the green hats, hop under the chute to a new place.

Lower the chute. Have the "leprechauns" put the hats on the edge of the chute. Start chanting at a faster pace. Pass the chute at that same speed. After a bit say, *"STOP."* Have those children put on the green hats. Raise the chute. Give these "leprechauns" a different command. Continue so that all the children have several opportunities to be "leprechauns."

Extension: Put green, white, and black paint at the easel.

102

GIANT UMBRELLA

By: Jane Flynn

Themes:
Spring
Rain
Weather

Body Position:
Squat/Stand

Hand Grip:
Thumbs-Down

Parachute Position:
Floor/Overhead

Parachute Movement:
Wave

Equipment:
Aluminum Foil Pan
Wooden Spoon

Warm-Up Exercise:
Balloon Float, 63

Relaxing Activity:
Did You Ever See a
    Lassie?, 126

Activity

Have the children squat around the chute and hold it, but not lift it up. Name several children to begin walking, running, skipping, etc. around the outside of the "umbrella" (chute).

After a little while, the adult should start making it "rain" by tapping the spoon on the aluminum pan. When the children hear the "rain," they should quickly stand up, lifting the "umbrella" up high. The children outside the "umbrella" should quickly run under it to keep dry. Say to them, *"I'm so glad you ducked under our umbrella. You didn't get wet!"* Those children take their places on the chute. Lower the chute. Play again and again.

Extension: Put sprinkling cans in the water table and encourage the children to "let it rain."

WIND STORM

Themes:
Spring
Weather
Wind

Body Position:
Stand

Hand Grip:
Thumbs-Down

Parachute Position:
Waist/Overhead

Parachute Movement:
Wave

Equipment:
Several Scarves

Warm-Up Exercise:
Merry-Go-Round, 58

Relaxing Activity:
Roll-Up, 131

Activity

Stand around the chute. Slowly start Waving it. Put several scarves under the chute.

Say, *"Woooooo"* like the blowing wind. When the children hear the wind, they should lift the chute over their heads and Wave it fast. As they are lifting the chute, name 2 or 3 children. They should run underneath the chute, pick up the scarves and run through the WIND STORM! Encourage all the other children to make the wind sound as they Wave the chute faster and faster.

When the children come out of the WIND STORM, calm down and lower the chute. Rest. Ask the children what it was like to be in a WIND STORM. Put the scarves back and play again.

Extension: Fill a large dish tub half full of water. Add 1/2 cup of Dawn® detergent. Give children straws and blow! *CREATE A TUB OF BUBBLES.*

COLORED EGG HUNT

Themes:
Easter

Body Position:
Sitting/Stand

Hand Grip:
Thumbs-Up

Parachute Position:
Waist/Overhead

Parachute Movement:
Taut

Equipment:
Colored Plastic Eggs
  Filled With Raisins,
  Cereal, etc.
Large Basket

Warm-Up Exercise:
Simon Says, 60

Relaxing Activity:
Did You Ever See a
  Lassie?, 126

Activity

Bring the basket of plastic eggs to the parachute. Sit around the chute. Hold up each egg and have the children call out its color. When finished, have the children stand and grab the parachute and raise it over their heads. Put the basket under the chute. Lower the chute.

Have the children raise the chute. Name a child (several children if a large group) to run under the chute, grab a certain color egg, and then run out. Lower the chute. Repeat until everyone has an egg. When parachute play is over, enjoy the snacks hiding in the eggs.

Extension: Have a tub of colored plastic eggs. Encourage the children to take them apart and put them back together.

WIGGLE WORM

Themes:
Spring
Worms

Body Position:
Kneel

Hand Grip:
Thumbs-Up

Parachute Position:
Waist

Parachute Movement:
Wave/Snap/Jerk

Equipment:
4' Piece of Clothesline

Warm-Up Exercise:
Simon Says, 60

Relaxing Activity:
Simon Says

Activity

Have the children pretend that the rope is a "worm." Give it to one child and have him put it on the parachute. Begin to slowly Wave the chute and watch the "worm" wiggle. Is it moving very fast? Wave the chute a little faster. How is the "worm" moving?

Now that the children can wiggle the "worm" all around the chute, play WIGGLE WORM. Name 3 children who are standing next to each other. Everyone else works together to wiggle the "worm" over to those children.

As the "worm" is moving, everyone chant *"Wiggle, wiggle, wiggle worm"* over and over until they wiggle the "worm" to those children. Continue playing WIGGLE WORM until he has visited all of the children.

After all this moving, WIGGLE WORM is pretty tired. Wiggle him gently towards the middle of the chute and through the hole to his underground home. (Another time play with several "worms.")

Extension: Look for real worms. Watch them wiggle and move.

SPRINGTIME FLOWERS

By: Jane Flynn

Themes:
Spring
Flowers

Body Position:
Squat/Stand

Hand Grip:
Thumbs-Down
(one hand)

Parachute Position:
Waist/Overhead

Parachute Movement:
Slow Wave

Equipment:
None

Warm-Up Exercise:
Exercise and Count, 62

Relaxing Activity:
Gunk, Gunk, 125

Activity

Have the children face in the same direction and squat around the parachute. Grab the edge of the chute with one hand. Start "walking" in a circle while singing SPRINGTIME FLOWERS. On the last line, *"They all pop up,"* jump up and wave the chute as high as you can.

Play again using 2 different flowers, maybe violets and mums.

> **SPRINGTIME FLOWERS**
> *(tune: Ring Around the Rosie)*
> by Jane Flynn
>
> Ring of Springtime flowers,
> Made from April showers.
>
> Tulips, buttercups
> They all pop up

Extension: Plant marigold seeds outside for everyone to enjoy as they come and go from school each day.

BEEHIVE

Themes:
Summer
Summer Creatures

Body Position:
Kneel

Hand Grip:
Thumbs-Up

Parachute Position:
Waist

Parachute Movement:
Flip-Flop

Equipment:
None

Warm-Up Exercise:
Copy Cat, 59

Relaxing Activity:
Wave and Sing, 124

Activity

Have the children kneel around the chute. Slowly Flip-Flop it. As the children move the chute, tell them to pretend that the parachute is a "beehive."

Name 5 children to crawl under the chute and pretend that they are the "bees" buzzing in the "hive." Have the rest of the children say BEEHIVE as they gently Flip-Flop the "hive." Instead of counting on the last line, call each bee's name. As each "bee" hears her name, she creeps out. Enjoy several times.

BEEHIVE

Here is the beehive
Where are the bees?
Hidden away where nobody sees.
Soon they come creeping out of the hive.
1, 2, 3, 4, 5.

Extension: Sing I'M BRINGING HOME A BABY BUMBLEBEE.

WHERE'S MY MOTHER?

Themes:
Summer
Animals
Animal Families

Body Position:
Sit

Hand Grip:
Thumbs-Up

Parachute Position:
Waist

Parachute Movement:
Taut

Equipment:
Pairs of Adult and Baby
 Farm Animals
Large Dish Tub

Warm-Up Exercise:
Bend and Touch, 62

Relaxing Activity:
Rock-A-Bye Baby, 127
(Use an animal from the game.)

Activity

Put all the animals in the dish tub. Have the children sit around the parachute. Show them the first pair of animals, such as the pig and piglet. Set the piglet next to you and give the pig to a child. Continue naming all the animals, and giving the adults to the children and keeping the babies.

Have the children hold the parachute. Say, *"Today we are going to pretend that our parachute is a barn roof. Lift it up high."* Everyone who has an animal should crawl under the roof, put it in the barn, and crawl back out. Lower the roof.

Hold up the baby cow and say, *"The calf is looking for its mom. Please help."* Give the calf to a child. Everyone else raises the barn roof and makes *"mooing"* sounds.

The child with the calf crawls under the roof, finds the mother cow, and puts the calf and mother together. The child takes his place on the chute. Lower the chute

Hold up another baby animal and continue until all the babies have found their moms.

Extensions:

1. Put the FARM ANIMALS in the block area.

2. Sing OLD McDONALD HAD A FARM often.

LET THE PARADE BEGIN

Themes:
Fourth of July
Celebrations
Parades

Body Position:
Stand

Hand Grip:
Thumbs-Up
(one hand)

Parachute Position:
Waist

Parachute Movement:
Wave

Equipment:
Recordings of Sousa
  Marches
(Change music depending on
  celebration.)
White Styrofoam Balls
  with Red and Blue
  Streamers Attached
(Change colors depending on
  celebration.)

Warm-Up Exercise:
Merry-Go-Round, 58

Relaxing Activity:
Rag Doll, 128

Activity

Have the children hold the parachute with both hands. Play a Sousa March. Everyone march in place to the beat of the music. Wave or Flip-Flop the chute as you march. Stop the music.

LET THE PARADE BEGIN! Have the children toss the decorated balls onto the chute. Everyone turn in the same direction and hold the chute with one hand. Begin the music, and march in a circle, Waving the chute as you do. Have fun watching the streamers fly into the air like gently moving "flags."

Stop the music again. Turn around. Start the music and march in the other direction, Waving your "flags" as you do.

Extension: March everywhere – to the playground, around the school, to the buses and cars, etc.

110

PARACHUTE FIREWORKS

Themes:
Fourth of July
Summer
Mexican Independence
Day

Body Position:
Stand

Hand Grip:
Thumbs-Up

Parachute Position:
Waist/Overhead

Parachute Movement:
Wave

Equipment:
½ sheets of All Colors
of Construction Paper

Warm-Up Exercise:
Balloon Float, 63

Relaxing Activity:
Good-Bye Balloons,
128

Activity

Have the children sit around the parachute. Give each child several sheets of paper. Have the children crumple up the paper into small tight balls and toss them on the chute.

After the "fireworks" have been made, have the children hold the edge of the chute and stand up. Everyone count, *"1, 2, 3, 4, 5 – Fireworks!"* As they shout, *"fireworks,"* everyone quickly Wave the chute high into the air and lower it, launching the "fireworks" into the sky.

Catch the "fireworks" as they come down. Collect those that flew off the chute. Count and launch more and more colorful "fireworks."

Extension: Talk about real fireworks the children have seen. Remember to include safety.

AUGUST

"DUNK" TANK

Themes:
Picnics
Toys

Body Position:
Sit

Hand Grip:
Thumbs-Up

Parachute Position:
Waist

Parachute Movement:
Wave

Equipment:
Lots of Sponge Balls
Large Pail

Warm-Up Exercise:
Exercise and Count, 62

Relaxing Activity:
Roll Up, 131

Activity

Have the children sit around the chute and hold it taut. Raise the chute. Give one child the pail. Have her crawl under the chute and put the pail under the hole. Crawl out and lower the chute.

Toss one sponge ball onto the chute. Have the children gently wave the chute, trying to "dunk" the ball through the hole so it lands in the "tank." Continue "dunking" the balls. Shout, *"Hooray!"* after you '"dunk" each one.

After all the balls have been "dunked," count how many balls landed in the "tank" and how many missed.

To make the game more challenging, put 2, 3, or 4 balls on the chute at once but only "dunk" one at a time. Try not to let any of the remaining balls roll off the sides. OR Use tennis balls. Remember, they roll very fast.

Extension: Play BOZO BUCKETS.

112

ROW YOUR BOAT

Themes:
Summer
Water Fun
Transportation

Body Position:
Sit

Hand Grip:
Thumbs-Down

Parachute Position:
Waist

Parachute Movement:
Wave

Equipment:
None

Warm-Up Exercise:
Parachute Pulls, 64

Relaxing Activity:
Are You Sleeping, 131

Activity

Have the children sit on each side of the chute. Start singing ROW, ROW, ROW YOUR BOAT. As they sing, have the children rock back and forth.

Sing again. Have several children stand up and pretend to row a boat around the "lake" (parachute). After singing and rowing for a little while, stop. Each rower should stop behind a nearby child. That child gets up and begins to row.

The first child takes his new place on the chute and begins to sing and rock with the group.

Continue playing, rocking back and forth, and singing at different speeds. The children who are rowing, must listen to the song and watch the chute to know how fast/slow to row.

Extension: Have small boats in the water table.

PICK ONE APPLE

Themes:
Johnny Appleseed Day
Fall
Fruit

Body Position:
Sit

Hand Grip:
Thumbs-Up

Parachute Position:
Waist

Parachute Movement:
Passing

Equipment:
Lots of Plastic Apples
or have the Children
Crumple Up Red Paper
Into "Apples"

Warm-Up Exercise:
Exercise and Count, 62

Relaxing Activity:
Wave and Sing, 124

Activity

Have the children sit around the parachute and hold it. Put all the "apples" on the chute.

Slowly start passing the chute around. As you are passing, sing PICK ONE APPLE. When you sing the last line, *"Pick it NOW,"* stop passing the parachute. Have each child pick an apple off the tree and put it behind her.

Start singing and passing the chute again. This time when you stop, say, *"All the boys pick an apple."* Next time all the girls. Next time those wearing red. Continue until all the apples have been picked.

Extension: Have an apple snack.

> **PICK ONE APPLE**
> *(tune: Mulberry Bush)*
>
> by Liz Wilmes
>
> Pick one apple off the tree,
> Off the tree, off the tree.
>
> Pick one apple off the tree,
> Pick it NOW! *(Shout "NOW")*

FALL COLORS

Themes:
Fall
Colors

Body Position:
Sit

Hand Grip:
Thumbs-Up

Parachute Position:
Waist

Parachute Movement:
Wave

Equipment:
Lots of Different Size
Fall Colored Pom-
Poms or Yarn Balls
Small Bushel Basket

Warm-Up Exercise:
Ripples and Waves, 65

Relaxing Activity:
Rock-A-Bye Baby, 127
(Could use a stuffed animal
squirrel.)

Activity

Have the children sit around the parachute and hold it. Raise the chute. Put the bushel basket underneath, but not in the middle. Lower the chute. Toss one pom-pom on the chute. Ask the children what color it is. (They call it out.)

Have all the children very slowly and purposefully Wave the chute so the pom-pom rolls to the hole and falls through. Name a child. Everyone else raise the chute over their heads. The child crawls under the chute, gets the pom-pom and puts it in the bushel basket. Lower the chute. Toss another pom-pom on the chute and play again – again – again until all the FALL COLORED pom-poms are in the basket.

Extension: Take a FALL COLOR WALK. Collect colorful leaves. Put the leaves and the basket of fall colored pom-poms on a large tray. Encourage the children to talk about and match the colors.

JACK-O-LANTERN ROLL

Themes:
Halloween
Fall
Pumpkins

Body Position:
Stand

Hand Grip:
Thumbs-Up

Parachute Position:
Waist

Parachute Movement:
Rolling Wave

Equipment:
4-5 Large Sponge Balls
  With Different Jack-
  O-Lantern Faces
  Drawn on Them

Warm-Up Exercise:
Balloon Float, 63

Relaxing Activity:
Breathe and Wave, 130

Activity

Put the jack-o-lantern sponge balls in a basket. Have the children stand and hold the chute. Lay one "jack-o-lantern" on the chute.

Encourage the children to work together and slowly roll JACK around the edge of the chute. (If it rolls to the middle, just bring it back to the edge.) Say, *"Stop."* The child nearest the "jack-o-lantern" grabs it and holds it up so everyone can see the face. Everyone call out how JACK feels. Have the child roll that "jack-o-lantern" under the chute. Put another JACK on the chute and play again.

Extension: Draw a giant JACK-O-LANTERN on a piece of orange posterboard. Cut it into 10-20 pieces. Put it on the floor for the children to put together over and over again.

116

RUN FAST LITTLE TURKEY

Themes:
Thanksgiving
Foods

Body Position:
Sit

Hand Grip:
Thumbs-Up

Parachute Position:
Waist

Parachute Movement:
Wave/Flip-Flop

Equipment:
None

Warm-Up Exercise:
Merry-Go-Round, 58

Relaxing Activity:
Breathe and Wave, 130

Activity

Sit around the parachute and teach your children RUN FAST LITTLE TURKEY. After they know the rhyme, have them pick up the chute.

Name several children to be the Pilgrims. They begin to walk together around the parachute looking for foods. The others slowly WAVE the chute and say the first 2 verses of RUN FAST LITTLE TURKEY.

When the children say, *"Then he saw a turkey, hiding in a log,"* point to another child who becomes the "turkey." That child gets up and quickly runs around the chute. The Pilgrims chase him. During the chase, the children Flip-Flop the chute and say the last verse.

Keep Flip-Flopping the chute until the "turkey" gets back to his place. Name several more "Pilgrims" and play again.

Extension: Say other turkey rhymes and fingerplays

RUN FAST LITTLE TURKEY
by Dick Wilmes

The brave little Pilgrim
Went out in the wood.
Looking for a meal
That would taste really
  good.

First he picked
  cranberries
Out in the bog.
Then he saw a turkey
Hiding in a log.

Run fast little turkey,
Run fast as you may,
Or you'll come to dinner
On THANKSGIVING DAY.

HELP MR. TURKEY FIND HIS FEATHERS

Themes:
Thanksgiving
Colors
Food

Body Position:
Stand

Hand Grip:
Thumbs-Down

Parachute Position:
Waist/Overhead

Parachute Movement:
Taut

Equipment:
Felt Turkey and
Different Colors and
Sizes of Feathers
Felt Board

Warm-Up Exercise:
New Places, 61

Relaxing Activity:
Roll Up, 131

Activity

Before playing, set the felt board next to you just outside the parachute. Have the children sit around the parachute. Show them the felt turkey. Put it in the middle of the felt board.

Give the boys all the turkey feathers. Have the girls raise the chute over their heads. Tell the boys to pretend they are turkeys and waddle under the chute and put the feathers on the floor and then waddle back to their places. Lower the chute.

Name several children. Tell each one what color and size feather to look for. Everyone else raise the chute and chant, *"Gobble – Gobble – Gobble – Gobble,"* etc. as the "turkeys" waddle under the chute, find their feathers, and waddle back to their places. Play again and again until the "turkeys" have found all the feathers.

Have the children lay the chute on the floor. Let the children put the felt feathers on the turkey. Call out the color.

Extension: Put the TURKEY FEATHER Game in Language.
DIRECTIONS: Enlarge the patterns. Make lots of different colors and sizes of turkey feathers. Make one turkey.

DECEMBER

JINGLE BELLS

Themes:
Christmas
Winter
Snow

Body Position:
Stand

Hand Grip:
Thumbs-Up

Parachute Position:
Waist

Parachute Movement:
Jerk

Equipment:
Large Jingle Bells

Warm-Up Exercise:
Parachute Pulls, 64

Relaxing Activity:
Are You Sleeping, 131
(Use bells again.)

Activity

Give each child several bells. Toss them onto the chute and sing JINGLE BELLS as they Jerk the chute in rhythm to the song. Sing again and Wave the chute in shallow ripples. How do the bells sound?

Extension: Sing JINGLE BELLS often.

DECEMBER

WRAPPING GIFTS

Themes:
December Holidays
Self Concept
Feelings

Body Position:
Sit

Hand Grip:
None

Parachute Position:
On Floor

Parachute Movement:
Taut

Equipment:
Small Toy for Each Child

Warm-Up Exercise:
Parachute Pulls, 64

Relaxing Activity:
Rock-A-Bye Baby, 127

Activity

Sit around the chute. Give 3-5 children a small toy. Have each child hold it up and tell what it is.

Everyone cover their eyes. Tap a child who has a gift on the head. That child should "wrap" his toy in the parachute. Everyone uncover their eyes and see if they can remember what gift just got wrapped up. Let the child "unwrap" his toy so everyone can see it.

Extension: Paint your own wrapping paper.

MITTEN MATES

Themes:
Winter
Winter Clothes

Body Position:
Sit

Hand Grip:
Thumbs-Down

Parachute Position:
Waist

Parachute Movement:
Taut

Equipment:
Pair of Mittens for Each Child

Warm-Up Exercise:
Exercise and Count, 62

Relaxing Activity:
Shhhh, 126

Activity

Have the children sit around the chute. Give each child a mitten from one of the pairs. Have each child put his mitten on.

Have the children raise the chute. Give the mitten mates to several children. Have them spread the mittens around under the chute. Lower the chute.

Have the children count, *"1, 2, 3, 4, 5, UP."* Raise the chute. Name 3-5 children. They should crawl under the chute, find the mate to the mitten they're wearing, put it on, and crawl back out.

Lower the chute. Play again and again until everyone has found his MITTEN MATE.

Extension: Put the MITTEN MATES Game on a table for the children to play during free choice.

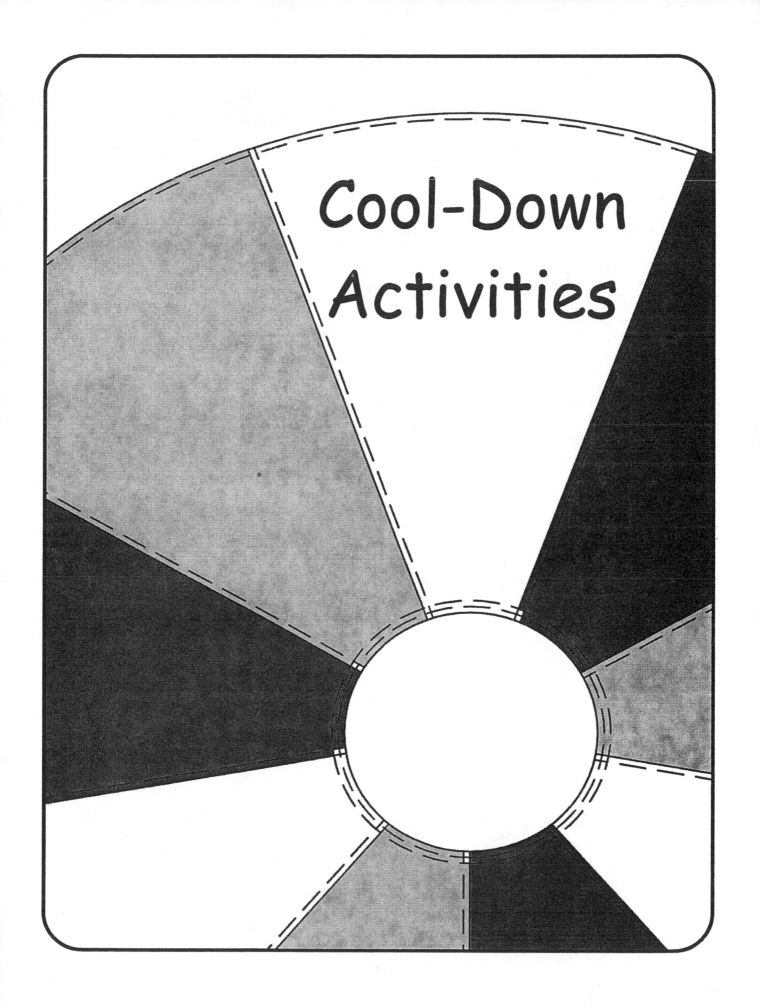

Cool-Down
Activities

WAVE and SING

Activity

Sit around the chute. In a slow, quiet voice, sing ROW, ROW, ROW YOUR BOAT, as you very gently wave your chute. Repeat several times, until everyone feels peaceful and quiet. Tiptoe the chute into a bunched-up position.

ROW YOUR BOAT

Row, row, row your boat
Gently down the stream.

Merrily, merrily, merrily, merrily,
Life is but a dream.

SIMON SAYS

Activity

Have the children sit on the floor and loosely hold the chute. Play a very short version of SIMON SAYS. Give the children 3-4 slow, quiet commands, such as:

"SIMON SAYS, 'Close your eyes'."

"SIMON SAYS, 'Take 3 deep breaths'."

"SIMON SAYS, 'Lay the parachute on the ground. Sit like a rag doll while I count to 10'." (Use a slow, quiet voice.)

Last Command
"SIMON SAYS, 'Crawl to the middle as you push the parachute into a bunched-up shape'."

GUNK, GUNK, WENT THE LITTLE GREEN FROG

Activity

Pretend that the parachute is a lily pad for GREEN FROG to rest on. Have the children sit, kneel, or stand around it. Quietly sing GUNK, GUNK WENT THE LITTLE GREEN FROG. As you sing, slowly Wave the "lily pad" to help GREEN FROG relax.

After the song quietly fold up the chute. FROG has fallen asleep. Shhh!

GUNK, GUNK, WENT THE LITTLE GREEN FROG

Gunk, gunk went the little green frog one day.
Gunk, gunk went the little green frog.

Gunk, gunk went the little green frog one day.
And his eyes went blink, blink, blink.

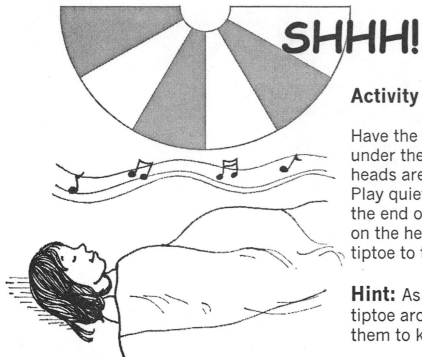

SHHH!

Activity

Have the children lie down and slip under the parachute so only their heads are showing. Close their eyes. Play quiet, calming music. Towards the end of the music, tap each child on the head. Have him sit up and tiptoe to the next activity.

Hint: As the children are resting, tiptoe around the chute, encouraging them to keep their eyes closed.

DID YOU EVER SEE A LASSIE?

Activity

Have the children sit around the parachute and loosely hold it. Begin swaying together. After you are in rhythm, sing DID YOU EVER SEE A LASSIE? As you sing *"this way"* everyone sway in one direction. When you sing *"that way"* sway in the other direction.

Continue singing and swaying using a quieter and quieter voice to the end. At the end you might only be moving your lips.

Shhh! Quietly scoot the chute into its bunched-up position.

**DID YOU EVER
SEE A LASSIE?**

Did you ever see a lassie
A lassie, a lassie,
Did you ever see a lassie
Go this way, and that?

Go this way, and that way
And this way, and that way.
Did you ever see a lassie
Go this way and that?

ROCK-A-BYE BABY

Activity

Have the parachute on the floor. Have the children stand around it. Put a doll baby (or teddy bear) in the middle of the chute. Have the children pick up the chute with a Thumbs-Down grip, holding it about waist high.

Very slowly begin to Jerk the chute, so you are gently rocking the baby. As you rock him, quietly sing the first verse of ROCK-A-BYE BABY. As you sing the second verse, continue to slowly Jerk the chute as you gently lower it to the floor.

Shhh! The baby is still sleeping, so be very quiet. Go around the circle and tap several children on the shoulders. Have them tiptoe their part of the parachute into the middle to cover up the baby. Tap the next several children to cover the baby. Continue until the whole parachute is covering the baby. (Remember to leave his face uncovered.)

ROCK-A-BYE BABY

Rock-a-bye baby on the tree top,
When the wind blows the cradle will rock.

When the tree breaks, the cradle will fall.
Down will come baby, cradle and all.

RAG DOLL

"Let your HEADS hang down like rag dolls."

"Let your SHOULDERS droop like rag dolls."

"Let your ARMS hang like rag dolls."

"Sit down and let your LEGS slump like rag dolls."

"I'll quietly count to 5, while you relax your WHOLE BODY like a rag doll. '1, 2, 3, 4, 5'."

"Push the chute to the middle like a relaxed rag doll."

Activity

Have the children stand around the chute. Encourage them to relax each part of their body. For example, you could say:

GOOD-BYE BALLOONS

Activity

Put several balloons on the parachute. Have the children hold the chute waist high. Gently Wave it. Whisper, *"Stop."* Take one balloon off the chute. Wave again. *"Stop."* Take another balloon off. Continue with this slow, quiet Wave until all the balloons are off the chute. Fold up the chute and quietly walk to the next activity.

Hint: This activity is easily adapted to any piece of equipment, such as beach balls, beanbags, or ropes that you have used with parachute games and exercises.

CLOSE YOUR EYES

Activity

Have the children sit around the chute and hold it with two hands. Ask them to close their eyes. Using a very quiet voice, count *"1, 2, 3, 4, 5"* as the children pull back as far as they can on the chute. Then count, *"5, 4, 3, 2, 1"* as they sit up again. Do this several times, each time getting quieter and slower.

Have the children open their eyes, stand up, and walk the chute to the middle. Hand it to you.

Shhhh!

Now the wiggles
Are out of us (Stand limp)
And we're as quiet
As quiet as can be (Finger over mouth)
Shhhh! (Very quietly)

BREATHE and WAVE

Activity

Have the children sit or stand. Start waving the chute in shallow, very slow movements. Breathe in as your arms move up, and out as your arms move down. Do this several times, going slower and slower and slower. Tiptoe the chute to the middle and lay it on the ground.

THIS OLD MAN

Activity

Have the children sit on the floor and loosely hold the chute. Slowly begin swaying side to side. When everyone is in rhythm, start humming THIS OLD MAN, as you sway. Hum several verses, getting quieter with each one.

> ### THIS OLD MAN
>
> *This old man, he played one,*
> *He played knick-knack on my thumb.*
> *With a knick-knack paddy-wack.*
> *Give your dog a bone.*
> *This old man came rolling home.*
>
> *This old man, he played two,*
> *He played kick-knack on my shoe....*
>
> *This old man, he played three,*
> *He played knick-knack on my knee...*
>
> *This old man, he played four,*
> *He played knick-knack on my door....*

Hmmm...
Hmmm...

ARE YOU SLEEPING?

You'll need

Lots of large jingle bells.

Activity

Have the children stand, kneel, or sit around the parachute. Put the bells on it. Gently jerk the chute side to side. Can you hear the bells? Sing ARE YOU SLEEPING.

ARE YOU SLEEPING?

Are you sleeping, are you sleeping
Brother John, Brother John?

Morning bells are ringing,
Morning bells are ringing,

Ding · ding · dong!
Ding · ding · dong!

ROLL UP

Roll Up

Activity

Have all the children kneel around the outstretched parachute and grab it Thumbs-Down. Begin to slowly roll up the parachute. As you are all rolling, slowly and quietly chant, *"Roll Up, Roll Up, Roll Up..."* When you get to the middle, everyone take a deep breath and let it out.

Hint: This is sometimes difficult because it takes hand strength and coordination. Remember to go slowly.

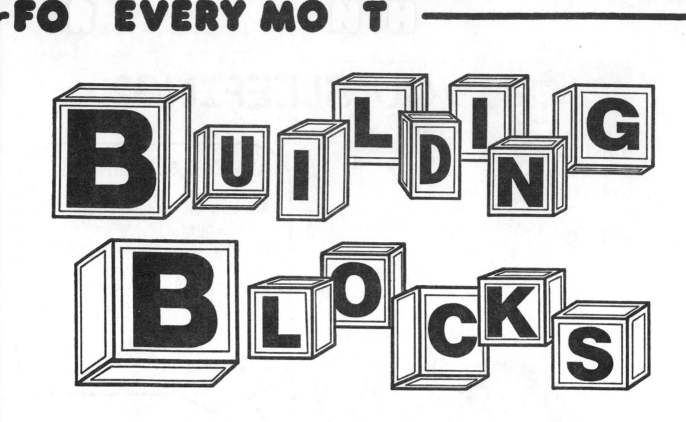

BUILDING BLOCKS Library

The Circle Time Series

by Liz and Dick Wilmes. Hundreds of activities for large and small groups of children. Each book is filled with Language and Active games, Fingerplays, Songs, Stories, Snacks, and more. A great resource for every library shelf.

Circle Time Book
Captures the spirit of 39 holidays and seasons.
ISBN 0-943452-00-7   **$ 12.95**

Everyday Circle Times
Over 900 ideas. Choose from 48 topics divided into 7 sections: self-concept, basic concepts, animals, foods, science, occupations, and recreation.
ISBN 0-943452-01-5   **$16.95**

More Everyday Circle Times
Divided into the same 7 sections as EVERYDAY. Features new topics such as Birds and Pizza, plus all new ideas for some popular topics contained in EVERYDAY.
ISBN 0-943452-14-7   **$16.95**

Yearful of Circle Times
52 different topics to use weekly, by seasons, or mixed throughout the year. New Friends, Signs of Fall, Snowfolk Fun, and much more.
ISBN 0-943452-10-4   **$16.95**

Paint Without Brushes

by Liz and Dick Wilmes. Use common materials which you already have. Discover the painting possibilities in your classroom! PAINT WITHOUT BRUSHES gives your children open-ended art activities to explore paint in lots of creative ways. A valuable art resource. One you'll want to use daily.
ISBN 0-943452-15-5   **$12.95**

Easel Art

by Liz & Dick Wilmes. Let the children use easels, walls, outside fences, clip boards, and more as they enjoy the variety of art activities filling the pages of EASEL ART. A great book to expand young children's art experiences.
ISBN 0-943452-25-2   **$ 12.95**

Everyday Bulletin Boards

by Wilmes and Moehling. Features borders, murals, backgrounds, and other open-ended art to display on your bulletin boards. Plus board ideas with patterns, which teachers can make and use to enhance their curriculum.
ISBN 0-943452-09-0   **$ 12.95**

Exploring Art

by Liz and Dick Wilmes. EXPLORING ART is divided by months. Over 250 art ideas for paint, chalk, doughs, scissors, and more. Easy to set-up in your classroom.
ISBN 0-943452-05-8   **$19.95**

CIRCLE TIME

ART

Magnet Board Fun

by Liz and Dick Wilmes. Every classroom has a magnet board, every home a refrigerator. MAGNET BOARD FUN is crammed full of games, songs, and stories. Hundreds of patterns to reproduce, color, and use immediately.
ISBN 0-943452-28-7   **$ 16.95**

Parachute Play, Revised

by Liz and Dick Wilmes. Play, wiggle, and laugh as you introduce children to the parachute. Over 150 holiday and everyday games for inside and outside play.
ISBN 0-943452-30-9   **$ 12.95**

Activities Unlimited

by Adler, Caton, and Cleveland. Hundreds of innovative activities to help children develop fine and gross motor skills, increase language, become self-reliant, and play cooperatively. This book will quickly become a favorite.
ISBN 0-943452-17-1   **$16.95**

Felt Board Fingerplays

by Liz and Dick Wilmes. A year full of fingerplay fun. Over 50 popular fingerplays, with full-size patterns. All accompanied by games and activities.
ISBN 0-943452-26-0   **$16.95**

Felt Board Fun

by Liz and Dick Wilmes. Make your felt board come alive. This unique book has over 150 ideas with patterns.
ISBN 0-943452-02-3   **$16.95**

Table & Floor Games

by Liz and Dick Wilmes. 32 easy-to-make, fun-to-play table/floor games with accompanying patterns ready to trace or photocopy. Teach beginning concepts such as matching, counting, colors, alphabet, sorting and so on.
ISBN 0-943452-16-3   **$19.95**

Learning Centers

by Liz and Dick Wilmes. Hundreds of open-ended activities to quickly involve and excite your children. You'll use it every time you plan and whenever you need a quick, additional activity. A must for every teacher's bookshelf.
ISBN 0-943452-13-9   **$19.95**

Play With Big Boxes

by Liz and Dick Wilmes. Children love big boxes. Turn them into boats, telephone booths, tents, and other play areas. Bring them to art and let children collage, build, and paint them. Use them in learning centers for games, play stages, quiet spaces, puzzles, and more, more, more.
ISBN 0-943452-23-6   **$ 12.95**

Play With Small Boxes

by Liz and Dick Wilmes. Small boxes are free, fun, and provide unlimited possibilities. Use them for telephones, skates, scoops, pails, beds, buggies, and more. So many easy activities, you'll want to use small boxes every day.
ISBN 0-943452-24-4   **$ 12.95**

Games for All Seasons

by Caton and Cleveland. Play with the wonder of seasons and holidays. Use acorns, pumpkins, be clouds and butterflies, go ice fishing. Over 150 learning games.
ISBN 0-943452-29-5   **$16.95**

2's Experience Series

by Liz and Dick Wilmes. An exciting series developed especially for toddlers and twos!

2's-Art
cribble, Paint, Smear, ix , Tear, Mold, aste, and more. Over 50 activities, plus lots f recipes and hints.

BN 0-943452-21-X

$16.95

2's-Sensory Play
Hundreds of playful, multi-sensory activities to encourage children to look, listen, taste, touch, and smell.

ISBN 0-943452-22-8

$14.95

2's-Dramatic Play
Dress up and pretend! Hundreds of imaginary characters...

ISBN 0-943452-20-1

$12.95

2's-Stories
xcite children with ory books! Read— xpand the stories th games, songs, d rhymes. Over 40 ooks with patterns.

BN 0-943452-27-9

$16.95

2's-Fingerplays
A wonderful collection of easy fingerplays with accompanying games and large FINGERPLAY CARDS.

ISBN 0-943452-18-X

$12.95

2's-Felt Board Fun
Make your felt board come alive. Enjoy stories, activities, and rhymes. Hundreds of extra large patterns.

ISBN 0-943452-19-8

$14.95

TODDLERS & TWO'S

BUILDING BLOCKS Subscription $20.00

2's EXPERIENCE Series
2'S EXPERIENCE - ART. 16.95
2'S EXPERIENCE - DRAMATIC PLAY 12.95
2'S EXPERIENCE - FELTBOARD FUN 14.95
2'S EXPERIENCE - FINGERPLAYS. 12.95
2'S EXPERIENCE - SENSORY PLAY. 14.95
2'S EXPERIENCE - STORIES 16.95

CIRCLE TIME Series
CIRCLE TIME BOOK 12.95
EVERYDAY CIRCLE TIMES. 16.95
MORE EVERYDAY CIRCLE TIMES 16.95
YEARFUL OF CIRCLE TIMES 16.95

ART
EASEL ART. 12.95
EVERYDAY BULLETIN BOARDS. 12.95
EXPLORING ART 19.95
PAINT WITHOUT BRUSHES 12.95

LEARNING GAMES & ACTIVITIES
ACTIVITIES UNLIMITED 16.95
FELT BOARD FINGERPLAYS 16.95
FELT BOARD FUN 16.95
GAMES FOR ALL SEASONS 16.95
LEARNING CENTERS. 19.95
MAGNET BOARD FUN 16.95
PARACHUTE PLAY, REVISED 12.95
PLAY WITH BIG BOXES. 12.95
PLAY WITH SMALL BOXES 12.95
TABLE & FLOOR GAMES 19.95

Prices subject to change without notice.

All books available from full-service book stores, educational stores, and school supply catalogs.

Check Our Website:
www.bblocksonline.com